SpringerBriefs in Computer Science

Series Editors
Stan Zdonik
Peng Ning
Shashi Shekhar
Jonathan Katz
Xindong Wu
Lakhmi C. Jain
David Padua
Xuemin Shen
Borko Furht
VS Subrahmanian

For further volumes:
http://www.springer.com/series/10028

Jenny Benois-Pineau • Frédéric Precioso
Matthieu Cord

Visual Indexing and Retrieval

 Springer

Jenny Benois-Pineau
Univ. Bordeaux
LABRI UMR 5800
Talence, France
jenny.benois@labri.fr

Frédéric Precioso
UNS
I3S UMR 7271/UNS_CNRS
Sophia Antipolis Cedex, France
precioso@polytech.unice.fr

Matthieu Cord
UPMC
LIP6 UMR 7606
matthieu.cord@lip6.fr

ISSN 2191-5768   ISSN 2191-5776 (electronic)
ISBN 978-1-4614-3587-7   ISBN 978-1-4614-3588-4 (eBook)
DOI 10.1007/978-1-4614-3588-4
Springer New York Heidelberg Dordrecht London

Library of Congress Control Number: 2012935105

Printed on acid-free paper

Springer is part of Springer Science+Business Media (www.springer.com)

Preface

Visual Indexing and Retrieval is a wide-scope research domain which unites researchers from image analysis and computer vision, to information management. For nearly twenty years, this research has been extremely active world-wide. With the advent of social networks conveying huge amount of visual information to the user, the ever increasing capacities of broadcast transmission of content via heterogeneous networks, popularization of hand-carried devices, the realm of possibilities has got wide open both for industry leaders and researchers. Indeed, the always increasing size of visual content databases has brought to the fore the need for innovative content understanding, retrieval and classification methods. Such methods are henceforth of paramount importance to let people the ability to exploit such huge databases.

The book is the result of joint efforts of the French research community joined through the GDR CNRS ISIS, the national academic network in the field. Thanks to this network, the research results gathered and explained in this book have received global recognition, and are gaining more and more success in technology transfer.

The authors hope that the most recent results and fruitful trends in Visual Indexing and Retrieval presented in this book will be helpful to young and experienced researchers willing to put the ideas forward and needing a solid understanding of the state-of-the art to do so, as well as to industry people willing to find an adequate algorithmic solution for their application area.

Acknowledgments: the authors acknowledge the governing board of GDR CNRS ISIS for supporting the project of this book.

Paris, France *Jenny Benois-Pineau*
January 2012 *Frédéric Precioso*
Matthieu Cord

Contents

Chapter 1
Introduction

Jenny Benois-Pineau, Frédéric Precioso, Matthieu Cord

1.1 Context and motivations

The research in visual information indexing and retrieval has become one of the most popular directions in the broad area of information technologies. The reasons for that are the technological maturity of capture, storage and network infrastructures, that allow for common daily-life capturing of images and recording of video with professional equipment and personal mobile devices. According to Internet sources the British Broadcasting Corporation set up team dedicated to process user-generated content, as an experimental group in April 2005 with 3 employees in the staff. The team was then made durable and got expanded, unveiling the integration of "citizen journalist" in the (broadcast) news mainstream. The same concept has been put in place by CNN that launched CNN iReport in 2006. This project was meant to allow CNN to collect user-generated news. So did the american Fox News with their 'uReport' project and the french BFM-TV broadcast channels. YouTube, Face-Book, FileMobile, DailyMotion, host and supply facilities for accessing a tremendous amount of professional and user-generated content for educational and entertainment purposes. The areas of societal activity such as video surveillance and security also generate thousands of tera-bytes of video content with specific issues to be tackled. Finally, the digitization and storage of cultural heritage be it Byzantine frescoes, Medieval miniatures, old manuscripts or feature films, documentaries and broadcasting programs or web-sites, lead to the production of a mass of visual data which has to be accessed and searched both by professionals for re-mastering and production of new visual content and by common users for various humanities research.

Thus, visual information indexing and retrieval has attracted a lot of research efforts since the early nineties [24]. However nowadays, owing to the size of large scale databases, complexity of visual interpretation tasks, the famous "semantic gap" between the (semantic) concept(s) the user is looking for in images and the digital representation of the (semantic) visual content, the research directions are widely open. This research field has been dramatically enriched by the last achievements in machine learning methods, the standardization of content descriptors and large-scale evaluation campaigns providing researchers with access to amounts of visual data associated to benchmarks for testing and evaluation. In this book, we propose a detailed review of the cutting-edge approaches in Visual Information Indexing, along with the original contributions of the authors of chapters.

1.2 Outline of the book

The book structure has naturally emerged from the key components of the visual indexing and retrieval problems. The next chapters, – Spatial and multi-resolution descriptions in visual indexing and – Machine learning approaches for visual information retrieval, are presenting the ingredients of the whole process. The next ones are dedicated to advanced considerations for the image representations, the scalability issues, and the evaluation.

Visual indexing and retrieval tasks always start with feature extraction from the raw data. Many approaches in several contexts have been developed since more than 30 years for now. Many primitives as Points of interest, regions, lines and so on, have been studied. Additionally, efficient descriptors are required. The Chapter 2 provides a deep overview of the basic feature extraction and description methods in the literature.

Representing these features at a higher semantic level description is the second stage of the process. The main steps for deriving image representation from visual local descriptors are described in Chapter 3. Well-known Bag-of-Visual-Words including recent extensions as sparse coding and spatial pooling methods are detailed. Higher semantic level data representation and similarity design are not independent but strongly related processes. Similarity measures between histograms, but also more complex functions such as kernels are presented. In order to address classification, retrieval or detection tasks, these similarities must be integrated into machine learning frameworks. We chose to focus on two major contributions from the Machine Learning community, namely Support Vector Machines and Boosting, very successful in multimedia retrieval applications.

Spatial structure is a key point in the building of the image representation. This information is usually ignored in basic representations. Advanced approaches try to overcome this drawback by adding spatial arrangements in the process. Furthermore, the natural willing to use information according to its visual importance and compressed-stream analysis yields multi-resolution approaches. In Chapter 4, integration of spatial context into visual description is deeply studied. Two trends on how to account for such information are considered. The first is the design of structural descriptors and integration of the spatial context in the signature matching. The second relates to the multi-resolution visual indexing.

Since image and video databases are becoming ever larger, scalability is definitely a critical requirement for visual information retrieval. The chapter 5 is dedicated to these scalability issues. The nature of the problems both for content-based retrieval and for mining are described. Main ideas and recent advances are presented, like the use of approximation or of shared-neighbour similarity. We also highlight some prospective directions, like embeddings, filtering based on simplified descriptions, optimization of content representations and distributed processing.

Finally, it is crucial to evaluate the visual indexing and retrieval methods and systems against common benchmark corpora. Having a deep understanding of the evaluation process is the best way to identify the strengths and weaknesses of the different approaches, and to trace promising ways to investigate. The chapter 6 gives an overview of the major evaluation campaigns and benchmarks for visual indexing and retrieval tasks. Data collection, relevance judgements, performance measures and experimentation protocols are discussed. The State-of-the-Art performance in recent campaigns and the lessons learnt from these campaigns are also presented.

Chapter 2
Visual feature extraction and description

Khalifa Djemal, Jean-Pierre Cocquerez, Frédéric Precioso

Abstract Since the very beginning of pattern recognition in the early 70's, pattern recognition remains a research challenge and has become of paramount importance nowadays. Today, machine learning methods complete expert knowledge in the choice of optimal feature sets with respect to image categories to be searched and recognized. This chapter provides an overview of the feature extraction and description approaches for still images as well as for spatio-temporal data analysis.

2.1 Introduction

Image recognition involves three distinct steps. Feature detection is the first step, aiming at identifying a set of image locations presenting with rich visual information. The second step is the feature description step consisting in defining robust descriptors based on the extracted features. The last step relates to the use of these descriptors for image representation, recognition and indexing. The next chapter 3 is dedicated to this step.

This chapter tries to give the reader an overview of the main recognition steps of detection and description. We present in section 2.2 the interest point detection approaches, point-based and region-based detectors. An extension to the spatio-temporal feature extraction is presented in section 2.2.3. In section 2.3, some reference feature descriptors are presented and discussed.

2.2 Visual primitive detection

The definition of a new interest point is related to two processes: (i) the detection of the exact localization of the point with specific characteristics as, for instance, a point the least similar to its neighbors (minimum of autocorrelation function) or a point of maximum of information (autocorrelation matrix with two high eigenvalues); (ii) and the description of the neighborhood of this point, related to color, texture or orientations of the gradient in the neighborhood. The quality of interest points can be evaluated trough the repeatability of both detection and description: how well interest point definition remains stable when submitted to any possible image transformations (rotation, crop, resizing for copy detection task) or stable to object category variations (points detected on car model are detected also on another model or brand, for classification task).

Historically, interest points detector and descriptor were first exploited for stereo-vision image matching, then for copy detection task (i.e. retrieving all copies of an original document even after quite strong geometric deformations). For such tasks, feature detectors must be very discriminant so as to ensure strong matching between similar points and quite sparse to be robust to occlusions. However, for classification task instead, the focus is put on generalization capabilities in order to retrieve similar content but under different views or in different contexts.

In the last ten years, many interst points detection mathods have been proposed. They can be distinguished either by their detection process or by their description process.

2.2.1 Point-based detectors

A wide variety of interest point detectors have been proposed in the literature [187]. They can be classified into two main categories: contour-based and intensity-based methods. Contour-based methods look for for maximal curvature or inflexion points along the extracted contour chains, or perform some polygonal approximation and then search for intersection points. Intensity-based methods compute a measure that indicates the presence of an interest point directly from the greyvalues.

To approximate the contours, Medioni et al.[143] use B-splines, interest points are maxima of curvature which are computed from the coefficients of thse B-splines. Horaud et al.[99] extract line segments from the image contours. These segments are grouped and intersections of grouped line segments are used as interest points. The algorithm of Pikaz and Dinstein [169] is based on a decomposition of noisy digital curves into a minimal number of convex and concave sections. The location of each separation point is optimized, yielding the minimal possible distance between the smoothed approximation and the original curve. The detection of the interest points is based on properties of pairs of sections that are determined in an adaptive manner, rather than on properties of single points that are based on a fixed-size neighborhood. In Mokhtarian and Suomela [148], the authors describe an interest point detector based on two sets of interest points. One set are T-junctions extracted from edge intersections. A second set is obtained using a multi-scale framework: interest points are curvature maxima of contours at a coarse level and are tracked locally up to the finest level. The two sets are compared and close interest points are merged.

Different intensity-based methods have been proposed for intersest points detection. Moravec [150] developed one of the first signal-based interest point detectors. His detector is based on the auto-correlation function of the signal. It measures the greyvalue differences between a window and windows shifted in several directions. Four discrete shifts in directions parallel to the rows and columns of the image are used. If the minimum of these four differences is superior to a threshold, an interest point is detected. Several interest point detectors [94, 72] are based on a matrix related to the auto-correlation function. The matrix (2.2) averages derivatives of the greylevel image in a window W around a point (x, y). This matrix captures the structure of the neighborhood. If this matrix is of rank two, that is both of its eigenvalues are large, an interest point is detected. A matrix of rank one indicates an edge and a matrix of rank zero a homogeneous region. Forstner in [72], uses the auto-correlation matrix to classify image pixels into categories, i.e., region, contour or interest point. Interest points are further classified into junctions or circular features by analyzing the local gradient field. This analysis is also used to determine the interest point location. Local statistics allow a blind estimate of signal-dependent noise variance for automatic selection of thresholds and image restoration.

2.2.1.1 Harris detectors

A large number of interest point detectors are based on high gradient detection as the well-known Harris [94] corner detector, i.e., detecting high gradients along two orthogonal directions in the image. The standard Harris corner detector satisfies some requirements: small number of points are detected only the interest one, these points are invariant to rotation, different sampling and to small changes of scale and small affine transformations. If we consider $I(x, y)$ the image function at point (x, y) can be similar to itself when it is shifted by $(\Delta x, \Delta y)$, this is can be given by the autocorrelation function:

$$c(x, y; \Delta x, \Delta y) = \sum_{(u,v) \in W(x,y)} w(u, v)(I(x, y) - I(u + \Delta x, v + \Delta y))^2 \quad (2.1)$$

Where $W(x, y)$ is a window centred at point (x, y) and $w(u, v)$ a Gaussian operator. Approximate the shifted function by the first-order Taylor expansion, and approximated by quadratic function become:

$$c(x, y; \Delta x, \Delta y) = [\Delta x \; \Delta y] \, Q(x, y) \begin{bmatrix} \Delta x \\ \Delta y \end{bmatrix} = [\Delta x \; \Delta y] \begin{bmatrix} A & B \\ B & C \end{bmatrix} \begin{bmatrix} \Delta x \\ \Delta y \end{bmatrix} \quad (2.2)$$

The second moment descriptor can be thought of as the covariance matrix of a two-dimensional distribution of image orientations in the local neighborhood of a point. Hence, the eigenvalues λ_1, λ_2, $(\lambda_1 \leq \lambda_2)$ of Q constitute descriptors of variations in I along the two image directions. Specifically, two significantly large values of λ_1 and λ_2 indicate the presence of an interest point. To detect such points,

Harris and Stephens [94] proposed to detect positive maxima of the corner function:

$$H = det(Q) - k.trace^2(Q) = \lambda_1 \lambda_2 - k.(\lambda_1 + \lambda_2)^2 \tag{2.3}$$

At the positions of the interest points, the ratio of the eigenvalues $\alpha = \lambda_2/\lambda_1$ has to be high. From (2.3) it follows that for positive local maxima of Q, the ratio α has to satisfy $k \leq \alpha/(1+\alpha)^2$. Hence, if we set $k = 0.25$, the positive maxima of Q will only correspond to ideally isotropic interest points with $\alpha = 1$, i.e $\lambda_1 = \lambda_2$. Lower values of k allow us to detect interest points with more elongated shape, corresponding to higher values of α. A commonly used value of k in the literature is $k = 0.04$ corresponding to the detection of points with $\alpha < 23$.

a)   b)

Fig. 2.1 Example of interest points detection by Harris detector on two different images.

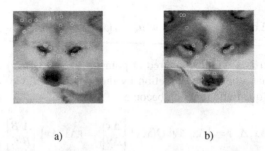

a)   b)

Fig. 2.2 Interest point detection by Harris detector on another kind of images.

Figures 2.1 and 2.2, show examples of interest points detection by Harris detector. Harris detector is unfortunately not stable against scale image variations.

2.2.1.2 Laplacian of Gaussian Family

In order to integrate scale invariance, most of interest point detectors are based on scale-space representation. The image $I(x,y)$ is convolved by a Gaussian kernel $G(x,y;\sigma)$ at a certain scale σ. The scale-space representation can be defined as follows:

$$L(x,y,\sigma) = \mathcal{G}(x,y,\sigma) * I(x,y) , \qquad (2.4)$$

also called *local jet*. The first multi-scale of interest point detector considers the scale-normalized Laplacian of the Gaussian (LoG) $\nabla^2_{norm}L(x,y;\sigma) = \sigma(L_{xx} + L_{yy})$ and detects scale-space maxima/minima, that are points simultaneously local maxima and minima of scale-normalized LoG with respect to both space and scale [131, 132]. This local maxima/minima of the scale-normalized Laplacian detection is also used for scale selection in other contexts, such as in corner detection, or scale-invariant feature transform [134].

From the fact that the scale-space representation L satisfies the diffusion equation, it follows that the Laplacian of the Gaussian operator can also be computed as the limit case of the difference between two Gaussian smoothed images (scale-space representations).

$$\sigma \nabla^2 G = \frac{\partial G}{\partial \sigma} \approx \frac{\mathcal{G}(x,y,k\sigma) - \mathcal{G}(x,y,\sigma)}{k\sigma - \sigma} \qquad (2.5)$$

The Difference of Gaussian (DoG) is a linear filter implemented in several artificial computer vision applications and used by a large variety of descriptors in image indexing and retrieval. It works by subtracting two Gaussian blurs of the image corresponding to different functions widths. The DoG operator can be seen as an approximation of Laplacian of Gaussians (2.5) and leads to the following equation:

$$(\mathcal{G}(x,y,k\sigma) - \mathcal{G}(x,y,\sigma)) * I(x,y) = L(x,y,k\sigma) - L(x,y,\sigma) \qquad (2.6)$$

The enhancing process with the DoG works in both spatial and frequency domains. Indeed, the performance of the filter is conditioned by the standard deviation of its two Gaussians.

2.2.2 Region-based detectors

To detect regions in the images, different approaches have been proposed in the literature [146]. Most detection methods are often based on pixels intensity, neighborhoods of contours or points of interest. Detected regions are subsequently used for 3D reconstruction or to define robust descriptors for content-based images retrieval systems. The image segmentation methods are often used as preprocessing methods, this ensures suitable detection. An extensive comparison between known region detectors has been proposed by Mikolajczyk et al. [146].

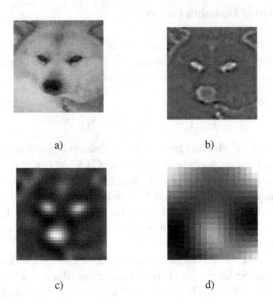

Fig. 2.3 DoG with different scales: a) Original image, b), c) and d) DoG with different octave and scales.

2.2.2.1 Image segmentation

Image segmentation is an essential preliminary step in the interpretation of images. It consists in partitioning the image in homogeneous areas corresponding to objects in the image. This score is based on image characteristics such as brightness, texture or color. There is no general solution to the problem of segmentation, but rather a set of mathematical tools and algorithms that can be combined to solve specific problems. In this context, edge detection plays an important role (see also section 2.3.1.4). Indeed, the contours often correspond to the limits of geometric objects in the scene. In almost all cases, edge detection, even sophisticated, produces an imperfect result. This is due to the presence of noise in the image, the difficulty of tunning the settings of the detector optimally, and the presence of variable contrast contours. Therefore, we can achieve only a segmentation based on contours. These are most often discontinuous or incomplete and many false contours are detected from noise or macroscopic textures. Various methods have been proposed as a remedy.

In general, it is possible to classify them into two main categories, direct approaches and model approaches. The direct approach is to extract from the image only relevant information, the model approach involves modeling the image or the desired objects. In the direct approach, we apply the operators working on the intensities of the image. In this category, can be cited the thresholding and its variants, mathematical morphological operations and low-level operations.

In the low-level operations, we find the linear filtering, such as convolution with a Sobel kernel type, Canny optimal filters, and the non-linear filtering, such as anisotropic diffusion. These operations lead to transformations of the image but do not allow the interpretation or modeling of information. From the knowledge that is available on the processed data, the model approach introduces in the segmentation process a priori information on the desired structures. It can be for example information about the shape of objects, their consistency, texture, environment and conditions for acquisition of the image. One can also distinguish between geometric models and the modeling of the image.

The geometric models used are the most active contour models [192, 34]. Among the model images, there are statistical models such as Markov fields and Bayesian process. Several studies conducted in the framework of active contours have given rise to two different approaches, the contour-based and region-based approaches. From these two main approaches, different methods have been proposed combining contours and regions information to better segment an object in an image [42, 58, 127].

Let us focus also on multiscale segmentation approaches delivering an image description as a hierarchy of partitions which are indexed by a scale parameter [88, 120]. Descriptors presented in this chapter can be applied on each partition. This is a manner to overcome scale invariance, with a counter part that is an increase of the feature vector size of images.

2.2.2.2 Intensity Extrema Based Region Detector

The intensity extrema based region detection method detects affine covariant regions through intensity extrema detected at multiple scales, then image exploration around them in a radial way, delineating regions of arbitrary shape which are then replaced by ellipses [211, 210]. For a given local extremum in intensity, the intensity function along rays emanating from the extremum is studied. The following function is evaluated along each ray:

$$f_I(t) = \frac{abs(I(t) - I_0)}{max\left(\frac{\int_0^t abs(I(t)-I_0)dt}{t}, d\right)} \tag{2.7}$$

with t an arbitrary parameter along the ray, $I(t)$ the intensity at position t, I_0 the intensity value at the extremum and d a small number which has been added to prevent a division by zero. The point for which this function reaches an extremum is invariant under affine geometric and linear photometric transformations (given the ray). Typically, a maximum is reached at positions where the intensity suddenly increases or decreases. The function $f_I(t)$ is in itself already invariant. Nevertheless, the points are selected where this function reaches an extremum to make a robust selection. Next, all points corresponding to maxima of $f_I(t)$ along rays originating from the same local extremum are connected to enclose an affine covariant region. This often irregularly-shaped region is replaced by an ellipse having the same shape moments up to the second order. This ellipse-fitting is again an affine covariant construction.

2.2.2.3 Maximally Stable Extrema Regions

In contrast with local interest points detectors of above methods, the Maximally Stable Extremal Regions (MSER) [142] is a local area-of-interest detector which denotes a set of distinguished regions, interest regions, that are detected in an image. All of these regions are defined by an extremal property of the intensity function in the region and on its outer boundary. The standard MSER algorithm detects bright homogeneous areas with darker boundaries (MSER+). The same algorithm can be applied to the negative of the input image, which results in a detection of dark areas with brighter boundaries (MSER-). In general, the combination of both sets is used to output the MSER detection result. The set of detected homogeneous regions with MSERs is closed under continuous geometric transformations and is invariant to affine intensity changes. Furthermore MSERs are detected at different scales.

2.2.3 Spatio-temporal extension

Many proposed methods deal with the detection of the spatio-temporal interest points. The importance of this kind of features has attracted the curiosity of researchers which have extended it to spatio-temporal detection especially for video analysis. Local image and video features have been shown successful for many recognition tasks such as object and scene recognition [68, 126] as well as human action recognition [125, 189]. Local space-time features capture characteristic shape and motion in video and provide relatively independent representation of events with respect to their spatio-temporal shifts and scales as well as background clutter and multiple motions in the scene. Such features are usually extracted directly from video and therefore avoid possible failures of other pre-processing methods such as motion segmentation and tracking.

In the literature, different spatio-temporal feature detectors [123, 156, 224] and descriptors [124, 125, 160] have been proposed. Feature detectors usually select spatio-temporal locations and scales in video by maximizing specific saliency functions. The detectors differ in the type and the sparsity of selected points. Feature descriptors capture shape and motion in the neighborhoods of detected points exploiting video characteristics such as spatial or spatio-temporal image gradients and optical flow.

The idea of the Harris interest point detector (section 2.2.1.1) is to find spatial location where the image has significant changes in both directions.
In this aim, to model a spatio-temporal image sequence Laptev [122] use a function $I : \Re^2 \longmapsto \Re$ and construct its linear scale-space representation $L : \Re^2 * \Re_+ \longmapsto \Re$ by convolution of I with an anisotropic Gaussian kernel with independent spacial variance σ_l^2 and temporal variance τ_l^2.

$$L(x,y;\sigma_l^2,\tau_l^2) = \mathcal{G}(x,y,\sigma_l^2,\tau_l^2) * I(x,y) \qquad (2.8)$$

Similar to the spatial domain 2.2, a spatio-temporal second-moment matrix is considered, that is a 3 by 3 matrix composed of first order spatial and temporal derivatives averaged using Gaussian weighting function.

$$Q = \mathcal{G}(x, y, \sigma_i^2, \tau_i^2) * \begin{bmatrix} L_x^2 & L_x L_y & L_x L_t \\ L_x L_y & L_y^2 & L_y L_t \\ L_x L_t & L_y L_t & L_t^2 \end{bmatrix} \tag{2.9}$$

where the integration scales σ_i^2 and τ_i^2 are related to the local scales σ_l^2 and τ_l^2 according to $\sigma_i^2 = s\sigma_l^2$ and $\tau_i^2 = s\tau_l^2$.

To detect interest points, Laptev et al. [125], search for regions in I having significant eigenvalues $\lambda_1, \lambda_2, \lambda_3$ of Q. Authors extend the Harris corner function (2.3) defined for the spatial domain to the spatio-temporal domain by combining the determinant and trace of Q as follows:

$$H = det(Q) - k.trace^3(Q) = \lambda_1 \lambda_2 \lambda_3 - k.(\lambda_1 + \lambda_2 + \lambda_3)^3 \tag{2.10}$$

Spatio-temporal interest points of I can be provided by detecting local positive spatio-temporal maxima in H.

In other proposed works, as a space-time extension of the Harris detector, Laptev et al. [123] proposed Harris 3D detector, they compute a spatio-temporal second moment matrix at each video point using independent spatial and temporal scale values, a separable Gaussian smoothing function and space-time gradient. The final spatio-temporal interest point detections are given by local maxima of matrix H. Willems et al. [224] proposed the Hessian detector as a spatial-temporal extension of the Hessian saliency measure for blob detection in images. The detector measures the saliency with the determinant of the 3D Hessian matrix. The position and scale of the interest point are simultaneously localized without any iterative procedure. The Cuboid detector was proposed by Dollar et al [59], this 3D detector is based on temporal Gabor filters. The interest point correspond to the local maxima of the response function. An evaluation of local spatio-temporal features for action recognition in [221], provides interesting details on the performance of these methods.

2.3 Descriptors

2.3.1 Feature spaces used by descriptors

Most description techniques are often based on universal feature such as color, texture, shape and edge. The description in these spaces can be achieved for example, by a simple operation as color averaging or by the determinant of the Hessian matrix in local shape space. In this section, we present different spaces.

2.3.1.1 Color

The feature natively coded at every pixel is the color. The color space in which the feature is coded has a big impact on its perceptual relevance. Most color features in the literature are based on other color spaces than standard RGB, like YUV, HSV, etc, which are considered as closer to human color perception [32]. Indeed, One of the main aspects of color feature extraction is the choice of a color space. Color features are relatively easy to extract, and efficient for indexing and retrieval in image databases. For example, color Histogram is the most commonly used color feature descriptor, its relatively invariance to position and orientation changes. The Color average descriptor [63] is generally defined in the RGB color space. Color autocorrelogram, defined in [102], captures the spatial correlation between identical colors. It is a subset of the correlogram [101] which explains how the spatial correlation of pairs of colors change with distance (similar to the cooccurrence matrix used for texture analysis of gray images).

2.3.1.2 Texture

Texture feature does not have an explicit definition but implicitly provides local distributions of pixel intensity analysis, thereby ignoring color information, in order to characterize spatial structures emerging from random visual primitives [77]. This lack of explicit definition entails the lack of uniqueness of a texture feature extractor and thus the lack of texture space to statically clusterize the feature space. We classify texture feature extractors in three different approaches:

- The features that are computed in the spatial domain, the first-order statistics and the cooccurrence matrix. The first-order statistics can be extracted from the normalized histogram of the image, by computing the Mean, the Standard Deviation, and the Coefficient of Variation. The co-occurrence matrix [115], called also the spatial gray level dependence matrices, counts how often pairs of gray level of pixels, separated by a certain distance and lying along certain direction, occur in an image. From these matrices, thirteen features related to the image texture, could be calculated. The most used descriptors can be extracted from these features: Average (or Mean), Variance, Signal to noise ration (SNR), Energy, Entropy, Contrast, Homogeneity, and Correlation [93].
- The features that are computed using model-based approach can only characterize textures that consist of micro textures [225].
- The features that are computed in a transform domain with multi-resolution approaches, such as for instance applying Daubechies wavelet, have gained wide interest over the years as they effectively describe both local and global information [114]. Wavelet texture features are the most important descriptors in this field. Texture features can be extracted from Daubechies wavelet coefficients of a two-level decomposition. The texture features are obtained by computing the sub-band energy of all wavelet coefficients (including the direction-independent

measure of the high-frequency signal information), after filtering the raw coefficients using Laplacian operator [191].

2.3.1.3 Shape

Shape descriptor is generally considered as some set of numbers that are produced to describe a given shape feature [147]. A descriptor attempts to quantify shape in ways that agree with human intuition. Good retrieval accuracy requires a shape descriptor to be able to effectively find perceptually similar shapes from a database. If a segmentation process provides regions representative enough of real semantic objects (section 2.2.2.1), new features requiring accurate object extraction can then be considered [33, 66]. Shape feature is up-to-now more used for segmentation task than for classification since it is bounded to precise shape detection in order to be relevant, except for very specific applications when the shape of objects to classify is easily available as for binary image classification for instance.

Many shape description and similarity measures have been developed in the literature [147]. A number of new techniques have been proposed lately. There are two main different approaches, contour- and region-based methods, and space and transform domains.

Contour-based methods and region-based methods [152] are the most common and general classification followed for instance in MPEG-7 standard. It is based on the use of shape boundary points as opposed to shape interior points. Under each class, different methods are further divided into structural approaches and global approaches. This sub-class is based on whether the shape is represented as a whole or represented by segments (2.2.2.1).

In this kind of approaches the shape feature extraction is generally based on gradient: shape context is based on the idea of picking n points on the contours of a shape. For each point on the shape, consider the $n-1$ vectors obtained by connecting the current point p to all other points. The set of all these vectors is a rich description of the shape localized at the current point p but is far too detailed. The key idea is that the distribution over relative positions is a robust, compact, and highly discriminative descriptor. So, the coarse histogram of the relative coordinates of the remaining $n-1$ points, is defined to be the shape context of the current point p. The bins are normally taken to be uniform in log-polar space. Translational invariance comes naturally to shape context and scale invariance is obtained by normalizing all radial distances by the mean distance between all point pairs in the shape [17, 18, 19].

In space domain, methods match shapes on point (or point feature) basis, while transform domain techniques match shapes on feature (vector) basis. The most common shape feature extraction approaches are based on the decomposition of the signal on a basis of functions as Legendre polynomial basis, B-spline, Zernike polynomial basis, Fourrier-Mellin polynomial basis. The most relevant decomposition coefficients are kept and stored in a vector (for Legendre moments, it has been experimentally shown that the first 40 moments are the most significant [73]).

2.3.1.4 Edge

Even though some recent works have been done on extracting edge information from images and representing this information through graphs of contours [199, 69, 158, 96, 95], most of the effort to define new local features has been put, in the last 5 years, on defining interest points to characterize even more atomic semantic primitives than regions (section 2.2).

The several edge descriptors are based on the extraction of gradient orientations, or local organization of gradients. Histogram of Oriented Gradient (HOG) descriptor [53] counts occurrences of quantized gradient orientations in localized portions of an image. Around a pixel, a dense local grid of uniformly spaced cells is defined. For each cell, a histogram of quantized gradient directions, or edge orientations, is compiled for the gradient pixels within the cell (orientation: $0°$, $45°$, $90°$, $135°$...). Histograms extracted from each cell of the grid are concatenated into one histogram which is the texture feature description of the pixel at central grid position.

In the 3D case, the HOG descriptor is based on histograms of 3D gradient orientation and can be seen as an extension of the SIFT descriptor to video sequence. Gradients are computed using an integral video representation. This descriptor combines shape and motion information at the same time.

2.3.2 Scale Invariant Feature Transform

Scale Invariant Feature Transform (SIFT) [134] is an approach for detecting and extracting local feature descriptors that are reasonably invariant to changes in illumination, image noise, rotation, scaling, and small changes in viewpoint. The Scale-space extrema detection represents the first main step for SIFT descriptor, this detection allows to obtain the keypoint localization. The orientation assignment and the generation of keypoint descriptors constitute the second main step. Interest points for SIFT features correspond to local extrema of DoG filters (section 2.2.1.2) at different scales (figure 2.3). The detection of interest points obtained by the convolution of the image with Gaussian filters at different scales, and the generation of DoG images from the difference of adjacent blurred images. The convolved images are grouped by octave (an octave corresponds to doubling the value of σ), and the value of k is selected so that we obtain a fixed number of blurred images per octave. This also ensures that we obtain the same number of DoG images per octave.

Interest points also called keypoints are identified as local maxima or minima of the DoG images across scales (figures 2.4.a and 2.5.a). Each pixel in the DoG images is compared to its 8 neighbors at the same scale, plus the 9 corresponding neighbors at neighboring scales. If the pixel is a local maximum or minimum, it is selected as a candidate keypoint to which is assigned an orientation. To determine the keypoint orientation, a gradient orientation histogram is computed in the neighborhood of the keypoint (using the Gaussian image at the closest scale to the keypoint's scale). The contribution of each neighboring pixel is weighted by the gradient magnitude and a

a) b)

Fig. 2.4 SIFT descriptor: a) Interest Points detection and b) An example of matching.

Gaussian window with a σ that is 1.5 times the scale of the keypoint. Peaks in the histogram correspond to dominant orientations. A separate keypoint is created for the direction corresponding to the histogram maximum, and to any other direction within 80% of the maximum value. Taking into account the keypoint orientation provides invariance to rotation.

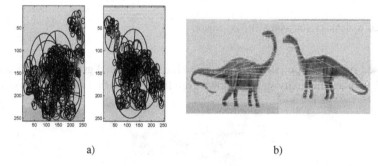

a) b)

Fig. 2.5 SIFT descriptor: a) Interest Points detection and b) An example of matching on different kind of images.

Once a keypoint orientation has been selected, the feature descriptor is computed as a set of orientation histograms on 4×4 pixel neighborhoods. The orientation histograms are relative to the keypoint orientation, the orientation data comes from the Gaussian image closest in scale to the keypoint's scale. Histograms contain 8 bins each, and each descriptor contains an array of 4 histograms around the keypoint. This leads to a SIFT feature vector with $4 \times 4 \times 8 = 128$ elements. This vector is normalized to enhance invariance to changes in illumination. SIFT features used in recognition tasks in large databases. Indeed, after SIFT descriptor computing on the input image, they matched to the SIFT features database (figures 2.4.b and 2.5.b).

The good performance of SIFT compared to other descriptors [145] is remarkable. Its mixing of crudely localized information and the distribution of gradient related features seem to yield good distinctive power while fending off the effects of localization errors in terms of scale or space. Using relative strengths and orientations of gradients reduces the effect of photometric changes.

2.3.3 Speeded Up Robust Features

The SURF descriptor, describes a distribution of Haar-wavelet responses within the interest point neighborhood. The integral image is exploited for speed. Moreover, only 64 dimensions are used, reducing the time for feature computation and matching, and increasing simultaneously the robustness. In [144, 132], authors present a new indexing step based on the sign of the Laplacian, which increases not only the matching speed, but also the robustness of the descriptor. The SURF descriptor

Fig. 2.6 Matching result with SURF descriptor.

is based on similar properties of localized information and gradient distribution as SIFT, with a complexity stripped down even further. The first step consists of fixing

Fig. 2.7 Matching result with SURF descriptor on different images.

a reproducible orientation based on information from a circular region around the interest point. Then, we construct a square region aligned to the selected orientation, and extract the SURF descriptor from this considered region [15]. Figures 2.6 and 2.7, present examples of matching results using SURF descriptor.

2.3.4 Global GIST descriptor

GIST descriptor was initially proposed in [157]. The idea is to develop a low dimensional representation of the scene, which does not require any form of segmentation. The authors propose a set of perceptual dimensions (naturalness, openness, roughness, expansion, ruggedness) that represent the dominant spatial structure of scene. They show that these dimensions may be reliably estimated using spectral and coarsely localized information. The image is divided into a 4x4 grid for which orientation histograms are extracted. Note that the descriptor is similar in spirit to the local SIFT descriptor [134].

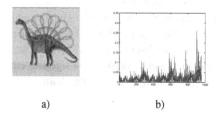

a)   b)

Fig. 2.8 GIST descriptor: a) Multiple scales of Fourier filter and b) resulting GIST descriptor.

The GIST descriptor has recently shown good description results for image search. In Li et al. [129], GIST is used to retrieve an initial set of images of the same landmarks, and then interest point based matching is used to refine the results and to build a 3D model of the landmark. In Hayes and Efros [97] it is used for image completion. Given a huge database of photographs gathered from the web the algorithm patches up holes in images by finding similar image regions in the database based on the GIST descriptor. Torralba et al. [209, 223] developed different strategies to compress the GIST descriptor. We show in figure 2.8, the resulting GIST descriptor.

2.4 Evaluation of feature detectors and descriptors

To evaluate the performances of feature detection and description methods, some techniques have been proposed in the literature [187, 221]. The ideal approach will be able to detect a large number of meaningful features in a given image, and will match them reliably across different views of the same object, as in the case of 3D reconstruction [151]. Critical issues in detection, description and matching are robustness to scaling, rotation and lighting changes. The main criteria used are repeatability and information content. These criteria generally measure the quality of the feature description for image matching, object recognition or 3D reconstruction [187]. In the case of image recognition in specific or heterogeneous image databases, feature selection methods are needed [116, 57, 56]. The evaluation efficiency is often conditioned by the used kind of image databases. Indeed, feature selection methods in some proposed works are based on the obtained performance for each feature, which is estimated by taking into account the recognition rate for a given images database [116].

2.5 Conclusion

In this chapter, we have presented the preliminary steps for any visual indexing and retrieval systems: feature detection and description. It is also fundamental for many different Computer Vision applications.

Well-known feature extraction schemes, like Harris and LoG detectors, and feature description approaches like SIFT and SURF have been presented. More general description like GIST were also discussed. CBIR system accuracy strongly depends on descriptor robustness to scaling, rotation and lighting changes. The exploitation of these descriptors in a global image processing chain is discussed in the next chapter.

Chapter 3
Machine learning approaches for visual information retrieval

Frédéric Precioso, Matthieu Cord

Abstract In this chapter, we first describe the main stages for deriving image representation from visual local descriptors which has been described in Chapter 2. Coding and pooling steps are detailed. We then remind briefly some of the most usual (dis-)similarity measures between histograms, paying a particular attention to a class of similarity functions, called kernels, we deeply investigate. We present several strategies to build similarity measures. These similarities can then either represent the basis of a similarity search system or be integrated into more powerful machine learning frameworks to address classification, retrieval or detection tasks.

3.1 Bag-of-Feature representations and similarities

As we have seen in the previous chapter, feature extraction usually lead to a set of unordered (local) feature vectors, called a Bag-of-Features (BoF), and visual content representation remains at a signal processing level. We would like to introduce more semantically rich representations and thus to be able to more accurately match data sharing perceptual characteristics and to better discriminate dissimilar data based on these semantic image representations.

Explicitly describing perceptual characteristics requires not only, first to extract relevant visual features, then to represent these features by a higher semantic level description, but also to define adequate (dis)-similarity functions between such data representations in order to evaluate the original perceptual similarity.

The standard processing pipeline for image representation is following three steps [29]: (i) local feature extraction, (ii) feature coding, and (iii) pooling in order to get the image descriptor. Classification algorithms (like support vector machines) are then trained on these descriptors.

Despite many feature detectors have been proposed to get salient areas, affine regions and points of interest [146], SoA methods for classification purpose usually carry out the feature extraction step using a uniform sampling over a dense grid on the image [41].

Let us denote the "Bag-of-Features" (BoF), *i.e.* the unordered set of local descriptors, by $\mathcal{X} = \{\mathbf{x}_j\}$, $j \in \{1,\ldots,N\}$, where $\mathbf{x}_j \in \mathbb{R}^d$ is a local feature and N the number of local regions or point of interest detected in the image. If we denote as $\mathbf{z}$ the final vector representation of the image used for classification, *i.e.* the "Bag-of-Visual-Words" (BoVW), the mapping from $\mathcal{X}$ to $\mathbf{z}$ can be decomposed into sequential coding and pooling steps [29]. The coding step consists in projecting local descriptors into a set of codebook elements, while the pooling step attempts at gaining some invariance by spatially aggregating the projected codes.

3.1.1 Bag-of-Visual-Words approaches (BoVW)

Inspired from text retrieval [229], visual dictionary-based approaches have been developed both to overcome the amount of data to be processed and to provide a relevant similarity between complex representations as BoFs.

As far as we know, Ma and Manjunath were the first to propose in their NETRA system [137] to exploit quantification properties of LBG algorithm on color pixels and to compute unsupervised visual dictionary. Later Fournier et al. [74] used Kohonen SOM map (on local Gabor feature vectors) to get the visual dictionary $\mathcal{C} = \{\mathbf{c}_m\}$, $\mathbf{c}_m \in \mathbb{R}^d$, $m \in \{1,\ldots,M\}$, where M is the number of visual words. **C** represents the matrix of all the center coordinates:

$$\mathbf{C} = \begin{bmatrix} c_{1,1} & \cdots & c_{1,k} & \cdots & c_{1,M} \\ \vdots & & \vdots & & \vdots \\ c_{l,1} & \cdots & c_{l,k} & \cdots & c_{l,M} \\ \vdots & & \vdots & & \vdots \\ c_{d,1} & \cdots & c_{d,k} & \cdots & c_{d,M} \end{bmatrix} \tag{3.1}$$

This strategy of building a visual dictionary to represent BoF by a unique vector, called Bag-of-Visual-Words (BoVW), has then be definitively popularized by the work of Sivic and Zisserman [200] applying this approach on Bags of SIFT. This is now the most used technique for BoF representation, implementing the two-steps pipeline: coding, pooling. The coding step can be modeled by a function $f\colon \mathbb{R}^d \longrightarrow \mathbb{R}^M$ as $f(\mathbf{x}_j) = \alpha_j$ (see Figure 3.1) which assigns a weight to the closest center $\mathbf{c}_m$ of the BoF vector $\mathbf{x}_j$ coded:

$$\alpha_{m,j} = 1 \text{ iff } m = \underset{k \in \{1,\ldots,M\}}{\operatorname{argmin}} \|\mathbf{x}_j - \mathbf{c}_k\|^2$$

When the weight $\alpha_{m,j}$ is constant, as above, the coding is called *hard coding* over the dictionary. The resulting binary code is very sparse. Alternatives to this standard scheme have been recently developed. Sparse coding [29, 228] modifies the optimization scheme by jointly considering reconstruction error and code sparsity:

$$\alpha_j = \underset{\alpha}{\text{argmin}} \|\mathbf{x}_j - \mathbf{C}\alpha\|_2^2 + \lambda \|\alpha\|_1$$

The strength of this approach is also that one can learn the optimal dictionary C while optimizing jointly over α. Efficient tools have been proposed to get tractable solutions [138].

Another extension to hard coding is the so-called soft coding [213] based on a soft assignment, that is to say $\alpha_{m,j}$ is not anymore a constant weight for all the vectors in the BoF but holds more precise information on the distribution of the BoF vectors over the visual dictionary such as, for instance, the distance (or the similarity) between the visual word $\mathbf{c}_m$ and the BoF vector $\mathbf{x}_j$. Resulting in a dense code vector, several in between hard and soft coding strategies – semi-soft coding – have been proposed, such as only considering in the soft code computation the distance between $\mathbf{x}_j$ and the k nearest neighbors visual words [133].

The second step for representing a BoF into a BoVW is the pooling step. Consider the pooling operator g: $\{\alpha_\mathbf{j}\}_{j\in 1,\dots,N} \longrightarrow \mathbb{R}^M$ as: $g(\{\alpha_j\}_j) = \mathbf{z}$ which aggregates the projections of all the BoF input feature vectors onto the visual dictionary to get a single scalar value on each row of the $\mathbf{H}$ matrix (Figure 3.1). Standard BoVW representation considers the traditional text retrieval pooling operator that is to say the *sum pooling*:

$$g(\{\alpha_j\}_j) = \mathbf{z} : \forall m,\ z_m = \sum_{j=1}^{N} \alpha_{m,j} \tag{3.2}$$

or the *max pooling* operator (when sparse coding strategy is performed):

$$g(\{\alpha_j\}_j) = \mathbf{z} : \forall m,\ z_m = \max_{j\in\{1,\dots,N\}} \|\alpha_{m,j}\| \tag{3.3}$$

$$\begin{array}{ccc} & & \begin{array}{ccccc} x_1 & & x_j & & x_N \end{array} \\ \mathbf{H} = & \begin{array}{c} c_1 \\ \\ c_m \\ \\ c_M \end{array} & \begin{bmatrix} \alpha_{1,1} & \cdots & \alpha_{1,j} & \cdots & \alpha_{1,N} \\ \vdots & & \vdots & & \vdots \\ \alpha_{m,1} & \cdots & \alpha_{m,j} & \cdots & \alpha_{m,N} \\ \vdots & & \vdots & & \vdots \\ \alpha_{M,1} & \cdots & \alpha_{M,j} & \cdots & \alpha_{M,N} \end{bmatrix} \Rightarrow g\text{: } \textit{pooling} \\ & & \Downarrow \\ & & f\text{: } \textit{coding} \end{array}$$

Fig. 3.1 BoVW: **H** matrix, with columns representing the coding operation and rows the pooling one.

The vector $\mathbf{z} \in \mathbb{R}^M$ is the final image representation. Among the extensions to the traditional pooling operator recently proposed, the Spatial Pyramid Matching (SPM) is the most powerful [126]: a fixed predetermined spatial image pyramid is computed and the previous pooling is operated over each block of the pyramid (see Section 4.2.1 of Chapter 4 for a detailed presentation). In [30], Boureau turned a corner by combining both SPM and local pooling over the codes which provides also a new perspective to other recent powerful approaches since VLAD [108] or Super-Vector Coding [232] appear then as specific pooling operations. In these aggregated methods, locality constraints are incorporated during the pooling step: only features belonging to the same clusters are pooled together.

Another BoVW improvement belonging to the aggregated coding class is the Fisher Kernel approach proposed by [165]. It is based on the use of the Fisher kernel framework popularized in [106] with Gaussian Mixture Models (GMM) estimated over the whole set of images. This approach may be seen as a generalization up to second order of the super vector approach [232] or to higher orders [167].

Such approaches finally reduce any data representation (how complex ever the initial data representation was) into one histogram over the visual dictionary. The idea is to define the explicit mapping of the BoF into the feature space defined by this codebook.

3.1.2 Vector distances and kernel functions

Up to a factor of normalization, a feature histogram is an approximation of the feature distribution, when the image is seen as a random variable.

The histogram representation has two drawbacks already mentioned in the previous section: such a representation does not preserve the spatial information (some solutions to overcome this limitation have already been mentioned in the previous section); the feature space quantization has a crucial impact on the size and the relevance of the feature histograms. Indeed, histogram comparison is commonly achieved through bin-to-bin distances, such as the l_1 and l_2 norms, based on the assumption of histogram domain alignment. However, this assumption is often violated when considering visual feature histograms owing to quantization, light changes, etc.

In their article [164], Pele and Werman clearly present the distances on histograms and their properties. As they pointed out, one way to provide robustness to bin-to-bin distances lies in modifying the number of bins: if bin number is low, the distance is more robust to alignment violations, but less discriminative; if bin number is high, the histogram distance is more discriminative, but less robust. Distances that account for cross-bin relationships (cross-bin distances) are of two kinds and can be both robust and discriminative:

The first type is distance of the form

$$D(P,Q) = \sqrt{(P-Q)^T \Sigma (P-Q)}$$

[91, 164] with P and Q two histograms and Σ the bin-similarity matrix. If the bin-similarity matrix is positive-definitive, then the distance D is a metric. When the

bin-similarity matrix Σ is the inverse of the covariance matrix, this distance is the Mahalanobis distance. If the bin-similarity matrix is the identity, then the distance is the l^2 distance and when the bin-similarity matrix is diagonal, the distance is called *"normalized euclidean distance"*.

The second type of distance that takes into account cross-bin relationships is the Earth Mover's Distance (EMD). EMD was defined by Rubner *et al.* [180] as the minimal cost that must be paid to transform one histogram (P) into the other (Q):

$$EMD^D(P,Q) = (\min_{\{F_{ij}\}} \sum_{i,j} F_{ij}D_{ij})/(\sum_{i,j} F_{ij}) \quad s.t. \quad F_{ij} \geq 0 \quad (3.4)$$

$$\sum_j F_{ij} \leq P_i, \quad \sum_i F_{ij} \leq Q_j, \quad \sum_{i,j} F_{ij} = min(\sum_i P_i, \sum_j Q_j) \quad (3.5)$$

where $\{F_{ij}\}$ denotes the flows. Each F_{ij} represents the amount transported from the ith supply to the jth demand. We call D_{ij} the ground distance between bin i and bin j. If D_{ij} is a metric, the EMD as defined by Rubner is a metric only for normalized histograms.

The above distance definitions are only valid if the two distributions have the same integral, as in normalized histograms or probability density functions. In that case, the EMD is equivalent to the 1st Mallows distance or 1st Wasserstein distance between the two distributions. Recently, Pele and Werman [163] proposed a modified version of EMD extending standard EMD to non-normalized histograms.

Since a feature histogram is an approximation of the unknown feature distribution, similarity measures on distributions are often applied to histograms as, for instance the Kullback-Leibler divergence, considering that these histograms are approximations of the same distribution. This assumption usually makes sense since the feature histograms to be compared are data representation outputs of the same feature extraction process (see Chapter 2).

In many histogram comparison situations, the difference between large bins is less important than the difference between small bins and should then be reduced. One can then normalize the feature vectors P and Q (z-score computation, for instance) before considering any standard distance. However some distances take this into account, such as the Chi-Squared (χ^2) distance :

$$\chi^2(P,Q) = \frac{1}{2}\sum_i \frac{(P_i - Q_i)^2}{(P_i + Q_i)}$$

The χ^2 histogram distance comes from the χ^2 test-statistic [203]. This is the traditional statistic for measuring the dependency between two variables (in a contingency table). It compares the observed frequencies with the frequencies that one would expect if there were no dependency between the variables. First introduced by LeBart *et al.* in [9] as a histogram measure in text retrieval context, χ^2-distance was successfully used for texture and object categories classification [186, 38, 83], local descriptors matching [71], shape classification [19, 92] and boundary detection [141]. The cross-bin χ^2 -like normalization reduces the effect of large bins having undo influence. Normalization was shown to be helpful in many cases, where the χ^2 histogram distance outperformed the l_2 norm.

In [65], Fauqueur presents a state of the art of most used similarity measures. Building new distances for histograms is still an active field of research which aims at improving histogram matching for classification as in [164].

Classically, $\mathcal{X}$, the space in which raw extracted visual features are defined, is called the *input space* (for instance, for feature vectors of dimension p, $\mathcal{X} = \mathbb{R}^p$). A kernel function k on $\mathcal{X} \times \mathcal{X}$ is a function which allows to evaluate similarity, correlation, between two data descriptions $\mathbf{x}, \mathbf{y} \in \mathcal{X}$. One of the definitions of kernels is: if we can find an embedding function ϕ (injection) which maps any data $\mathbf{x}$ to a vector $\phi(\mathbf{x})$ in a Hilbert space (*induced space* or *feature space*), then the function k defined by the following dot product in the induced space:

$$k(\mathbf{x}, \mathbf{y}) = < \phi(\mathbf{x}), \phi(\mathbf{y}) > \tag{3.6}$$

is a kernel function over $\mathcal{X}$ [196]. The embedding function ϕ can either be explicitly or implicitly defined. This definition also provides two ways to build a kernel function k either by exhibiting the mapping function ϕ or starting from an existing valid kernel function k' and modifying its mapping function ϕ', with respect to bilinear properties of dot product, in order to design the final mapping function ϕ of k.

This definition is also the reason for the growing interest for kernel functions: since a kernel is a dot product (in an induced space), it ideally replaces dot products in decision making algorithms (as regression, classification / neural networks, support vector machines...) that linearly estimate a decision function providing these algorithms with non-linear decision function estimation capability. Furthermore, with this new non-linear potential these algorithms have been extremely successful at a wide variety of supervised and unsupervised Machine Learning tasks: for instance, using the string kernel Distant Segments, Boisvert *et al.* [25] have obtained the best results, until now, for the problem of HIV-1 co-receptor usage prediction. Because of this special adequateness with kernel functions, these algorithms have been gathered under the name *kernel machines* (see Section 3.2.1).

A kernel function k can equivalently be defined through a dot product eq.(3.6) or as a semi-definite positive function: a kernel k is symmetric over $\mathcal{X} \times \mathcal{X}$ and verifies:

$$\forall \{\mathbf{x_i}\}_{i=1...n} \in \mathcal{X}, \forall \{\alpha_i\}_{i=1...n} \in \mathbb{R}, \sum_{i=1}^{n} \sum_{j=1}^{n} \alpha_i \alpha_j k(\mathbf{x}_i, \mathbf{x}_j) \geq 0 \tag{3.7}$$

An easy way to verify if a kernel is positive, consists in insuring that all eigenvalues of its Gram Matrix are positive. Given a set of vectors $\{\mathbf{x_i}\}_{i=1...n} \in \mathcal{X}$, the Gram matrix K of a kernel k is the n dimensional matrix such that: $K_{ij} = k(\mathbf{x}_i, \mathbf{x}_j)$.

Among the most popular kernels, let us mention:

- Gaussian RBF kernel: $k(\mathbf{x}, \mathbf{y}) = \exp^{-\frac{\|\mathbf{x} - \mathbf{y}\|^2}{2\sigma^2}}$
- Polynomial kernel: $k(\mathbf{x}, \mathbf{y}) = (\mathbf{x} \cdot \mathbf{y} + 1)^q$

- Gaussian χ^2-kernel: $k(\mathbf{x}, \mathbf{y}) = \exp^{-\frac{\chi^2(\mathbf{x},\mathbf{y})}{\sigma}}$

Histogram intersection is a similarity measure between two color histograms which has been proposed by Swain and Ballard [205] for color indexing. Let us use the same notation as in Barla et al. [12] for A and B the histograms of the images A_{im} and B_{im}. Both histograms consist of m bins, and the ith bin for i = 1,...,m is denoted with a_i and b_i respectively. Let us assume that A_{im} and B_{im} have the same size (N pixels); by construction we have $\sum_{i=1}^{m} a_i = N$ and $\sum_{i=1}^{m} b_i = N$. Then:

$$\mathcal{I}(A,B) = \sum_{i=1}^{m} min(a_i, b_i) \qquad (3.8)$$

In [12], the authors proved that histogram intersection $\mathcal{I}^A$ is a kernel by expanding the histogram A into a $N \times m$-dimensional binary vector $\mathbf{A}$ defined as

$$\mathbf{A} = (\overbrace{1,1,...,1}^{a_1}, \underbrace{0,0,...,0}_{N-a_1}, \overbrace{1,1,...,1}^{a_2}, \underbrace{0,0,...,0}_{N-a_2}, ..., \overbrace{1,1,...,1}^{a_m}, \underbrace{0,0,...,0}_{N-a_m}) \qquad (3.9)$$

and similarly B with $\mathbf{B}$.

The histogram intersection $\mathcal{I}(A,B)$ in Eq.(3.8) can be readily written as the standard inner product between the two corresponding vectors $\mathbf{A}$ and $\mathbf{B}$:

$$\mathcal{I}(A,B) = \mathbf{A} \cdot \mathbf{B} \qquad (3.10)$$

In the case of images of different sizes, the above holds by setting the dimension of $\mathbf{A}$ and $\mathbf{B}$ to $M \times m$ where M is the maximum size of any input. As noted in [87], this binary encoding only serves to prove positive-definiteness and is never computed explicitly.

3.1.3 Bag-of-Features (BoF) similarity and retrieval

In the previous section, we have described similarity measures when each data is represented by a single vector which highly reduces the amount of vectors to be compared. However, Bag-of-Features (BoF) showed to be more powerful when information retrieval targets object categories, especially when the categories are related to objects which cover only a (small) part of the data (image or video) and that feature vectors should then represent very local descriptions.

Let image I_j be represented by a feature bag B_j composed of s unordered vectors $\mathbf{b}_{sj} \in \mathbb{R}^p$: $B_j = \{\mathbf{b}_{sj}\}_s$. Let $\mathcal{B}$ the database of images and $\mathcal{F}$ the database of feature vectors $\mathbf{b}$. Let I_q be a query image represented by a bag $B_q = \{\mathbf{b}_{rq}\}_r$. In the context

---

[A] In [12] Barla et al. called the histogram intersection kernel K_{int} and work on non-normalized histograms. The notation $\mathcal{I}$ has been further introduced when considering intersection between normalized histograms. For the sake of clarity, we only keep the notation $\mathcal{I}$ in this book.

of database ranking, denoting $score_j = score(I_q, I_j)$ the score between the query image I_q and image I_j, the retrieval process in the database $\mathcal{B}$ can be written as:

$$\underset{I_j \in \mathcal{B}}{Sort}(score_j) \tag{3.11}$$

Several strategies have been proposed to define the score $score_j$ which can be formally written as:

$$score_j = \sum_{\mathbf{b}_{rq} \in B_q} \sum_{\mathbf{b}_{sj} \in B_j} f(\mathbf{b}_{rq}, \mathbf{b}_{sj}) \tag{3.12}$$

where f is a similarity function that reflects the similarity between two descriptors $\mathbf{b}_{rq}$ and $\mathbf{b}_{sj}$. The main strategies are detailed in the next subsections.

Let us introduce the general notation:

$$f_{\mathcal{P}}(\mathbf{x}, \mathbf{y}) = \mathbb{1}_{\mathcal{P}(\mathbf{x}, \mathbf{y})} \tag{3.13}$$

where $\mathbb{1}_{\mathcal{P}(\mathbf{x}, \mathbf{y})}$ is the indicator function that takes the value 1 when the predicate $\mathcal{P}$ is true and 0 otherwise.

3.1.3.1 Voting-based Strategy

The principle of the voting method is to search, in the feature database $\mathcal{F}$, the nearest neighbor vectors of the r vectors $\mathbf{b}_{rq}$ from the query image I_q. Each feature vector $\mathbf{b}_{sj}$ which is among the k nearest neighbors of one of the query PoIs $\{\mathbf{b}_{rq}\}$, increases by 1 the score $score_j$ representing the similarity score of the image I_j with the query I_q (*i.e.* $\mathbf{b}_{sj}$ "votes" for I_j as similar to the query I_q).

In the framework of eq.(3.12) using notation of eq.(3.13), for a voting strategy based on R Nearest Neighbors (RNN) search algorithm f is defined as:

$$f(\mathbf{x}, \mathbf{y}) = f_{RNN}(\mathbf{x}, \mathbf{y}) = \mathbb{1}_{d(\mathbf{x}, \mathbf{y}) \leq R} \tag{3.14}$$

where $d(., .)$ is a distance (or dissimilarity measure) defined in the descriptor space. This voting measure is symmetric. For instance, SIFT descriptors which are 128-dimensional feature vectors, are typically compared using Euclidean distance and R has often been set to 200 in our experiments.

An other strategy consists in using a k Nearest Neighbors (kNN) search algorithm:

$$f(\mathbf{x}, \mathbf{y}) = f_{kNN}(\mathbf{x}, \mathbf{y}) = \mathbb{1}_{\mathbf{x} \in kNN(\mathbf{y})} \tag{3.15}$$

where $f_{kNN}(\mathbf{x}, \mathbf{y}) = 1$ only if $\mathbf{x}$ is among the k Nearest Neighbors of $\mathbf{y}$. It has to be noticed that this similarity measure is not symmetric.

The voting techniques met a big success in computer vision community for copy detection task. Lowe [134] provided not only an algorithm for both extraction and description of unordered sets of SIFT PoIs to represent image content, but also a two-step retrieval technique of (locally) similar images: a fast kNN search for each PoI from the query, then a voting strategy to rank the images of the database with respect to the number of "matching votes" to the query. However, such techniques only count the number of "good" matches between images, considering all matches as equivalent. This provides robustness to occlusion in copy detection context but is a drawback for similarity search task. A more semantic-oriented matching would then account for matching accuracy but also matching impact.

Jegou *et al.* [107] showed that the use of a visual dictionary for image retrieval can be interpreted as a voting strategy which matches individual descriptors with a nearest neighbors (NN) search algorithm. The codebook construction defines a quantizer Q that is formally a function:

$$Q : \mathbb{R}^d \rightarrow [1,k] \\ \mathbf{x} \longmapsto Q(\mathbf{x}) \tag{3.16}$$

that maps a local descriptor $\mathbf{x} \in \mathbb{R}^d$ to an integer index referred to a codeword. The quantifier $Q(\mathbf{x})$ is then the index of the closest codeword to the descriptor $\mathbf{x}$.

Using notations of eq.(3.13) and eq.(3.16), the similarity function f between two descriptors is defined as:

$$f(\mathbf{x},\mathbf{y}) = f_Q(\mathbf{x},\mathbf{y}) = \mathbb{1}_{Q(\mathbf{x})=Q(\mathbf{y})} \tag{3.17}$$

Note that the score $score_j$ obtained by using this similarity function in eq.(3.12) still corresponds to the dot product between two BoW vectors [107].

When huge database are considered, computation time and memory become a real issue. If sparse, BoVW features can be computed very efficiently using an inverted file. These aspects are discussed in Chapter 5.

3.1.3.2 Kernel on Bag-of-Features

Projecting data onto a visual dictionary, as good as it could be, is not a lossless compression process. Richer representations may be investigated.

One of the main properties of kernel functions is to provide similarity between data from non-metric spaces, even from non-vector spaces. Among complex data structures, BoFs as sets of vectors (allowing repeated vectors) $B_i = \{b_{ri}\}_r$ belong to the set of subsets $Parts(\mathcal{B})$ which is not a vector space. Let us denote $\Phi : Parts(\mathcal{B}) \rightarrow \mathcal{H}$ the embedding function which maps any bag B_i to a vector $\Phi(B_i)$ in a Hilbert space $\mathcal{H}$. To design kernels over sets, one can define a function K corresponding to a dot product in the induced space:

$$K(B_i,B_j) = < \Phi(B_i), \Phi(B_j) > . \tag{3.18}$$

One classic kernel on bags is defined in [197]:

$$K(B_i, B_j) = \sum_{b_{ri} \in B_i} \sum_{b_{sj} \in B_j} k(b_{ri}, b_{sj}), \tag{3.19}$$

where k is the minor kernel function on $b_{ri} \in B$. If we define by Φ the embedding function into the feature space $\mathcal{H}$, we have in this case: $\Phi(B_j) = \sum_{b_{rj} \in B_j} \phi(\mathbf{b}_{rj})$.

This approach can be seen, in the formalism of eq.(3.12), as a voting approach with $score_j = K$ and where the hard-assignment f_{RNN} or f_{kNN} is replaced with a soft-assignment k. In other words, instead of increasing the score $score_j$ for good matches, all matches are considered but they are weighted regarding their influence on the matching of the two bags.

The function of eq.(3.19) is semi-definite positive (see [197], Chap. 9 for proof), however it returns the average similarity between all the local descriptors which may smooth good match impact in presence of too noisy data.

In order to increase the high matches $k(b_{ri}, b_{sj})$, Lyu [136] introduces the following kernel function:

$$K_{lyu}(B_i, B_j) = \frac{1}{|B_i|} \frac{1}{|B_j|} \sum_{b_{ri} \in B_i} \sum_{b_{sj} \in B_j} k(b_{ri}, b_{sj})^q. \tag{3.20}$$

Using a high value of q, high matches are increased much more than low matches.

One step further has been done by Grauman and Darrell [87] who designed a kernel function, the pyramid match kernel, to compute the optimal partial matching between BoFs of variabled-size. This kernel takes into account the distribution of PoIs in the feature space through a multi-level hierarchical block matching. At the finest level, the feature space is clustered such that each unique d-dimensional feature vector falls into its own cluster. At the next level, the side length of the cells is doubled. This step is repeated until all feature points fall into the same unique cell. At a resolution level, the clustering is mapped to an histogram: each clustering cell corresponding to one bin of the histogram. The whole multi-resolution clustering is thus mapped to a multi-resolution histogram pyramid. Let $\mathbf{X} = \mathbf{x}_1, \mathbf{x}_2, ..., \mathbf{x}_m$ with $x_i \in \mathbb{R}^d$ be a BoF, at one resolution level the histogram stores the distribution of feature vectors from X. The feature extraction function Ψ for an input feature vector BoF $\mathbf{X}$ is defined as:

$$\Psi(\mathbf{X}) = [H_0(\mathbf{X}), ..., H_{L-1}(\mathbf{X})] \tag{3.21}$$

where $L = \lceil log_2(D) \rceil + 1$, D is the maximal range between any two feature vectors in the feature space, $H_i(\mathbf{X})$ is a histogram vector formed over points in $\mathbf{X}$ using d-dimensional bins of side length 2^i, and $H_i(\mathbf{X})$ has a dimension $r_i = (\frac{D}{2^i})^d$.

The pyramid match $\mathcal{P}_\Delta$ measures similarity (or dissimilarity) between point sets based on implicit correspondences found within this multi-resolution histogram space. The similarity between two input sets $\mathbf{Y}$ and $\mathbf{Z}$ is defined as the weighted sum of the number of feature matchings found at each level of the pyramid formed by $\mathbf{Y}$:

$$\mathcal{P}_\Delta(\Psi(\mathbf{Y}), \Psi(\mathbf{Z})) = \sum_{i=1}^{L} \frac{1}{d2^i} (\mathcal{I}(H_i(\mathbf{Y}), H_i(\mathbf{Z})) - \mathcal{I}(H_{i-1}(\mathbf{Y}), H_{i-1}(\mathbf{Z})) \quad (3.22)$$

where $H_i(\mathbf{Y})$ and $H_i(\mathbf{Z})$ refer to the ith histogram in $\Psi(\mathbf{Y})$ and $\Psi(\mathbf{Z})$ respectively, and the difference under the sum between the two intersection kernels provides the number of newly matched pairs at level i. A new match is defined as a pair of features that were not in correspondence at any finer resolution level. Speedup kernel ranking scheme may be performed using approximate kNN search [40]. In [85], Grauman extended this scheme to a vocabulary-guided pyramid using a visual dictionary on PoIs, thus compacting BoFs. See Chapter 5 for a detailed presentation of the scalability issues.

All these works illustrate the power of kernel representation for similarity, dealing with non-vector spaces and fitting in most efficient machine learning algorithms.

3.2 Learning algorithms

Visual representations and similarities are used in more general data processing chain in order to address classification, retrieval or detection problems. All of them are performing decision processes that usually include learning.

Machine Learning has boomed for 20 years now. We focus in this section on two learning strategies – SVM and Boosting – that have been very successful for the last decade. SVM and Boosting strategies are used in various research and engineering areas, from text categorization to face recognition. They are commonly used as learning algorithm for classification and retrieval for their effectiveness [216, 105].

3.2.1 Support Vector Machines

SVM is a supervised learning method originally used for binary classification and regression [216]. They are the successful application of the kernel idea [5] to large margin classifiers [215] and have proved to be powerful tools. We briefly give optimization scheme details and solvers are discussed. See [51] for a comprehensive introduction to Support Vector Machines.

Optimization formulation

Using kernel notations previously defined (*cf. Eq 3.6*), the classifiers we are considering here, associate classes $y = \pm 1$ to data descriptions or patterns $x \in \mathcal{X}$ by first mapping the data into feature vectors $\phi(x)$ in an induced space and taking the sign of a linear discriminant function f depending on two parameters w and b:

$$f(x) = \langle w, \phi(x) \rangle + b \tag{3.23}$$

Thanks to the *Reproducing Kernel* theory [7], the function f may be written as a *kernel expansion*: $f(x) = \sum_{i=1}^{n} \alpha_i k(x, x_i) + b$ and w as linear combination of the training data in the induced space: $w = \sum_{i=1}^{n} \alpha_i \phi(x_i)$. Examples such that $\alpha_i \neq 0$ are called *Support Vectors*.

For many linear decision methods, parameters w and b are determined using a set of n training examples $(x_1, y_1) \cdots (x_n, y_n)$ and an optimization criterion. Support Vector Machines (SVM) [89] are a linear classifier that separates the training set with the widest margin (distance to the hyperplane of the closest points on both side) in the feature space induced by the kernel function k.

As the distance between any pattern x and the hyperplane is $\frac{yf(x)}{\|w\|}$, the hard margin SVM optimization may be easily formulated as:

$$\min_{w,b} \frac{1}{2} \|w\|^2 \quad \text{subject to} \quad \forall i, \quad y_i f(x_i) \geq 1 \tag{3.24}$$

As explained in [50], if the data are noisy, it is interesting to allow some examples to violate the margin constraint. The resulting optimization scheme is the soft margin version of the SVM. Introducing the slack variables ξ_i, the l1-norm Soft SVM minimizes the following objective function in feature space:

$$\min_{w,b} \frac{1}{2} \|w\|^2 + C \sum_{i=1}^{n} \xi_i \quad \text{subject to} \quad \forall i \quad y_i f(x_i) \geq 1 - \xi_i \text{ and } \xi_i \geq 0 \tag{3.25}$$

When compared to a l2-norm algorithm (on ξ variables), l1-norm scheme is less sensitive to outliers in training data. For very large values of the hyper-parameter C, this expression minimizes $\|w\|$ (i.e. maximizes the margin) under the constraint that all training examples are correctly classified (all the ξ_i equal to zero). This is exactly the hard margin problem. For small C, ξ_i are no more forced to zero, and this constraint relaxation (soft margin) is decisive to get good results on noisy data.

An another way to express the optimization problem requires the hinge loss function ℓ defined as $\ell(y_i f(x_i)) = \max(0, 1 - y_i f(x_i))$. Using ℓ, the optimization problem of equation 3.25 is equivalent to:

$$\min_{w,b} \frac{1}{2} \|w\|^2 + C \sum_{i=1}^{n} \ell(y_i f(x_i)) \tag{3.26}$$

When the induced space is a finite dimensional space, it is possible to solve this primal formulation of the optimization problem. Otherwise, learning SVM can be achieved by solving the dual of this convex optimization problem. The standard formulation is defined as:

$$\max_{\alpha} \sum_{i=1}^{n} \alpha_i - \frac{1}{2} \sum_{i,j} y_i y_j \alpha_i \alpha_j k(x_i, x_j) \quad \text{subject to} \quad \forall i \begin{cases} \sum_i \alpha_i y_i = 0 \\ 0 \leq \alpha_i \leq C \end{cases} \tag{3.27}$$

Solvers

Efficient numerical algorithms have been developed to solve the dual SVM optimization formulation. It may be expressed as a dual Quadratic Programming problem. The best known methods are the Conjugate Gradient method [214] and the Sequential Minimal Optimization (SMO) [170]. Both methods work by making successive searches along well chosen directions. Some famous SVM solvers like SVMLight [109] or SVMTorch [49] propose to use decomposition algorithms to define such directions. Each direction search solves the restriction of the SVM problem to the half-line starting from the current vector α and extending along a specified direction. For SMO, Platt [170] observes that direction search computations are much faster when the coefficients of the search direction u are almost zero. To ensure the constraints $\sum_k u_k = 0$, the SMO algorithm uses search directions whose coefficients are all zero except two (a single $+1$ and a single -1). The state-of-the-art implementation of SMO is libsvm [35].

The use of a linear kernel (or a explicit mapping) simplifies the SVM optimization problem. w may be explicitly expressed avoiding the kernel expansion anymore, and the kernel matrix computation. Computing gradients of either the primal or dual cost function is very cheap making linear optimization very interesting for large scale databases.

Recent work exhibits new algorithms scaling linearly in time with the number of training examples. SVMPerf [110] is a simple *cutting-plane* algorithm for training linear SVM converging in linear time for classification. LibLinear [64] also reaches very good performances on large scale datasets, converging in linear time with an efficient dual coordinate descent procedure.

Solving linear SVM in the primal can also be very efficient. Stochastic Gradient Descent (SGD) approaches [28] usually obtain the best generalization performances (pegasos [194], svmsgd [27]). Many details and comparisons of large scale SVM optimization methods may be found in [26] that deeply inspired the writing of this section. SGD implementation has been used by the winners of the PASCAL VOC large scale challenges 2010 and 2011 [61].

SVM have been very successful and are very widely used because they reliably deliver state-of-the-art classifiers with minimal tweaking.

3.2.2 Multiple Kernel Learning for feature combination

The *Bag Of Words* model previously introduced, (including spatial information detailed in Chapter 4), proved to reach state of the art performances in many image categorization tasks. However, it is still a very challenging task because most descriptors present strong intra-class variabilities and inter-class correlations. Designing efficient feature combination strategies is way to improve classification performances that has been extensively studied in the 2000s. Multiple Kernel Learning(MKL) [10] is now widely used in machine learning applications as an alternative

method for combining multiple features, thanks to the availability of efficient algorithms [175, 39]. It is also a very hot topic in Computer Vision community where
the visual feature combination problem is very challenging for classification tasks
(see for instance the workshop on Kernels and Distances for Computer Vision at
ICCV 2011). Different features are obtained by projection of local descriptors on
a visual codebook, and MKL strategies used to optimize their combination [218].
MKL offers the possibility to jointly learn the weighting of the different channels
(features and similarity kernels) and the classification function [11]. The goal is to
find the optimal classification function f defined as follows:

$$f(x) = \sum_i \alpha_i y_i \sum_m \beta_m k_m(x, x_i) - b \tag{3.28}$$

where the variable to be optimized are both the α and the w. Efficient algorithms
exist for solving the related optimization convex problem [174].

Recent works attempting at using MKL on image datasets for combining different channels [219, 79] use MKL optimization algorithms based on ℓ_1 norm to
regularize the kernel weights, like SimpleMKL [174]. Since this leads to sparse
solutions, most studies report that MKL is often outperformed by simple baseline
methods (product or averaging) [219, 79]. However, especially in Computer Vision
context, the different kernels are generated from different visual modalities, most of
them being informative and many of them being complementary (*e.g.* edge, color
and texture). Therefore, it is more interesting to find a proper weighting between
them than performing kernel selection. There exists however ℓ_2 MKL optimization
schemes [119] to solve the MKL problem, but except [227], there has been few
attempt to apply these schemes on image databases to find a non-sparse combination of complementary descriptors. An hybrid strategy [168] aims at learning a
non-sparse combination between different image modalities, but still using a ℓ_1 optimization algorithm. The idea is to generate for each descriptor numerous kernels
by varying their parameters (*e.g.* standard deviation σ for gaussian kernels). For
each channel c, M kernels $K_{c,\sigma}$ are considered, and few of them are selected using
a ℓ_1 MKL strategy (corresponding to a σ parameter selection). This adapted MKL
problem formulation leads to find the optimal function of the form:

$$f(x) = \sum_{i=1}^{N_e} \alpha_i y_i \sum_{c=1}^{N_c} \sum_{\sigma=\sigma_1}^{\sigma_M} \beta_{c,\sigma} k_{c,\sigma}(x, x_i) - b \tag{3.29}$$

where the joint optimization is performed on α_i (N_e parameters) and $\beta_{c,\sigma}$ ($N_c \times$
M parameters). This approach allows to jointly learn individual kernel parameters
σ and kernel combination coefficients β_m. The sparse solution output by ℓ_1 MKL
algorithms is therefore used as an option to cross-validation. Other approaches like
ℓ_2 MKL use a two-step procedure: optimal σ is first determined by cross-validation,
and combining the kernels is then performed for a fixed σ. This leads to a sub-
optimal parameter estimation with respect to the global optimization scheme.

More general combinations than MKL have been proposed by Varma et al. with
a gradient descent based learning algorithm named GMKL [217].

3.2.3 Boosting

The concept of Boosting was introduced in 1995 by Freund [75]. As described in [105], *"Boosting is a way of combining the performance of many "weak" classifiers in order to produce a powerful "committee", by sequentially applying a classification algorithm to re-weighted versions of the training data and then taking a weighted majority vote of the sequence of classifiers thus produced"*. For many classification algorithms, this simple strategy results in dramatic improvements in performance. Boosting algorithm uses weak classifiers (error rate $\delta < 0.5$) of a priori knowledge to build a strong classifier.

Algorithm 1 Boosting basics

Parameters: h_t weak learners
Input: A set $\mathcal{A}$ of examples (training data) with labels $\mathcal{Y} = \{-1, +1\}$
Initialization: All examples have the same weight
for $t = 1$ to T **do**
    Use h_t with $\mathcal{A}$ and current weight distribution
    Increase weights of misclassified examples at current iteration
end for
Output: H a majority weighted vote of all h_t

In 1996 Freund and Schapire propose the AdaBoost (Adaptive Boosting) algorithm allowing to choose automatically weak assumptions with adjusted weight. AdaBoost does not depend anymore on a priori knowledge [76]. Here is a concise description of AdaBoost in the two-class classification setting (**Algorithm 1**). We define $H(\mathbf{x}) = \sum_1^T \alpha_t h_t(\mathbf{x})$ where each $h_t(\mathbf{x})$ is a classifier producing values $+1$ or -1 and α_t are constants; the corresponding prediction is $sign(H(\mathbf{x}))$. The AdaBoost procedure trains the classifiers $h_t(\mathbf{x})$ on weighted versions of the training samples from $\mathcal{A}$, giving higher weights to cases that are misclassified at current iteration. This is done for a sequence of weighted samples, and then the final classifier is defined to be a linear combination of the classifiers from each stage.

Let us first present the most common boosting algorithm for classification context: Discrete AdaBoost (**Algorithm 2**).

Other versions differ from the Discrete AdaBoost algorithm by modifying one, some or all the following steps in the (**Algorithm 2**): 3:, 4:, 5:, 6: and 7:.

- Real AdaBoost (1998): weak learner returns a class probability estimate $p_m(\mathbf{x})$. The contribution to the final classifier is half the logit-transform of this probability estimate.
- GentleBoost (1998): modified version of Real AdaBoost using Newton stepping rather than exact optimization of p_m at each step.
- LogitBoost (2000): additive logistic regression model
- BrownBoost (2001): examples far from boundary are considered as noise and thus decreased in weight
- FloatBoost (2003): remove the worst WeakLearners at each iteration

---

Algorithm 2 AdaBoost (Discrete AdaBoost)

E_w represents the expectation over the training data with weights $\mathbf{w} = (w_1, w_2, \ldots, w_N)$, and $\mathbb{I}_S$ is the indicator of the set S. At each iteration, AdaBoost increases the weights of the observations misclassified by $h_t(\mathbf{x})$ with a factor that depends on the weighted training error.

1: **Initialization:** Start with weights $w_i = 1/N, i = 1, \ldots, N$.
2: **for** $t = 1, 2, \ldots, M$ **do**
3:     Fit the classifier $h_t(\mathbf{x}) \in \{-1, +1\}$ using weights w_i on the training data.
4:     Compute $err_t = E_w[\mathbb{I}_{(y \neq h_t(\mathbf{x}))}]$.
5:     $\alpha_t = log((1 - err_t)/err_t)$.
6:     Set $w_i \leftarrow w_i \, exp[\alpha_t \, \mathbb{I}_{(y_i \neq h_t(x_i))}]$, $i = 1, 2, \ldots, N$.
7:     renormalize w_i so that $\sum_i w_i = 1$.
8: **end for**
9: **Output: the classifier** $sign[H(\mathbf{x}) = \sum_{m=1}^{M} \alpha_t h_t(\mathbf{x})]$

- JointBoost (2004): multi-class boosting, jointly train N binary classifiers sharing same features

Many other AdaBoost versions are available dedicated to specific configurations (noise, multi-class problem, etc).

Let us present apart a boosting algorithm quite different from above versions of AdaBoost. Indeed, even if RankBoost is a classification Boosting based algorithm, the purpose of this learning method is to classify data against each other with respect to a rank of classification (**Algorithm 3**)[B]. The algorithm takes the outline of AdaBoost but replaces the examples by pairs (positive examples against negative examples). The selection aims at maximizing the score of positive examples compared to that of negative examples. The dataset is then ranked by sorting H values.

3.2.4 Linear Programming Boosting (LPBoost) for Multiple Kernel Learning (MKL)

As detailed in section 3.2.2, MKL has proved to be a very efficient way to combine multiple features. Among all the methods, the LP-β approach proposed by Gehler and Nowozin [78] has been for a long time the most efficient algorithm, even though very recently Orabona et al. [159] proposed a new MKL formulation and a fast stochastic gradient descent method that solves this novel MKL formulation. Gehler and Nowozin interpret the MKL decision function as a convex combination of F SVMs (denoted f_m) and propose several formulations based on LPBoost algorithm [55] in order to optimize the β coefficients in eq.(3.28). Among these formulations, their LP-β algorithm consistently outperforms all other considered methods

---

[B] As for boosting, other schemes different from classification framework have been recently proposed. They focus on optimizing the ranking instead of classification error [212].

Algorithm 3 RankBoost

Parameters: h_t weak learners

Input: A set $\mathcal{A}$ of examples (training data) with labels $\mathcal{Y} = \{-1, +1\}$ {
lets denote i_p positive example index and i_n negative example one.}

Initialization: Set example distribution with $D_1(i_p, i_n) = \frac{1}{n_p * n_n}, i = 1, \ldots, m$, with $n_p =$
$\#\{positive\ examples\}$ and $n_n = \#\{negative\ examples\}$

for $t = 1$ to T **do**

  Find the weak learner h_t which maximize classification score r_t with respect to example difficulty D_t,

$$r_t = \arg\max_{h_t \in \mathcal{H}} \sum_{i_p, i_n}^{m} D_t(x_{i_p}, x_{i_n})[h_t(x_{i_p}) - h_t(x_{i_n})]$$

  Choose $\alpha_t \in \mathbf{R}$ the weight of the weak learner so that $\alpha_t = \frac{1}{2} \log \frac{1+r_t}{1-r_t}$

  Update weights of training example pairs: $D_{t+1}(x_{i_p}, x_{i_n}) = \frac{D_t(x_{i_p}, x_{i_n}) e^{-\alpha_t (h_t(x_{i_n}) - h_t(x_{i_p}))}}{Z_t}$ with Z_t
  a normalization factor.

end for

Output: $H(\mathbf{x}) = \sum_{t=1}^{T} \alpha_t h_t(\mathbf{x})$

---

at the time. In their boosting framework, adding more learners comes with a reasonable additional cost since it only scales linearly in F, furthermore any trained weak learner can be reused.

The two step training procedure arguably is less principled than a joint optimization eq.(3.28): Ideally there would have enough data to adjust f_m and β on independent sets. Since this is usually not the case, the authors propose the following two stage scheme to avoid biased estimates.

First they perform model selection using 5 fold cross-validation to select the best hyperparameters for each SVM f_m individually (i.e. at least the SVM standard regularization parameter C_m). At this point the only parameter left is the hyper-parameter ν from LPBoost formulation [55] which trades the smoothness of the resulting function with the hinge loss on the points, analogously to the SVM standard regularization parameter. Since there is no independent training data left to set this parameter they compute for each f_m the cross-validation outputs using its best regularization parameter identified before. This results in a prediction for each training point using a classifier which was not trained using that point (but on other percentage of the training data). The cross-validation outputs of all SVMs f_m are used as training data for LP-β. They perform cross-validation to select the best parameter ν and subsequently train the final combination β.

The main concern using this scheme, is that the input to the LP-β training is not from the classifier f_m later used in the combination. However it is reasonable to assume that the learners used to produce the training data for LP-β are not too different. The experiments validate this assumption as there is no overfitting for the LP-β model. Owing to the two training stages most of the training can be done in parallel with each piece being reasonably fast.

Most results, Gehler and Nowozin obtained, turn out to be disadvantageous for the classic MKL formulation because the f_m kernels on their own are already discriminative. It should be pointed out that from the experiments and the conclusion of Gehler and Nowozin, the kernel combination baseline methods average and product, should always be considered as canonical competitors to MKL and included in any study using MKL. With LP-β, they derive a method that yields better performance, is equally fast and leads to sparse multiclass object classification systems.

3.2.5 Interactive learning

In classification task, Machine Learning algorithms aim at learning a statistical estimation of a classification function f_A using examples (or training data) in order to predict the proper label of any data. Let $\mathcal{X} = \{\mathbf{x}_i\}_{1,n}$ be the n image indexes of the database. A training set is expressed as a subset of $\mathcal{X}$ provided with valid labels: $\mathcal{A} = \{(\mathbf{x}_i, y_i)_{i=1,n}\}$. The classifier is then trained using these labels, and a classification function f_A is determined. The set of unlabeled data is denoted by $\mathcal{U} = \{(\mathbf{x}_i, y_i)_{i=1,n} \mid y_i = 0\}$.

The classification function f_A is usually defined as a linear combination of basic functions which are evaluated on (all) examples from the training set $\mathcal{A}$. The definition of this combination coefficients and the definition of the basic functions depend on what is the decision issue targeted: classification, retrieval, etc., and how the decision is taken: Support Vector Machines, Boosting, etc.

In classification task, the whole training set is involved in building the decision function, usually defined by the sign of classification function, which determines the class label to unlabeled data.

Retrieval task is usually considered as a binary classification: the relevant class, the set of images corresponding to the user query concept, and the irrelevant class composed by the remaining in the database. The above training set becomes then $\mathcal{A} = \{(\mathbf{x}_i, y_i)_{i=1,n} \mid y_i \neq 0\}$ where $y_i = 1$ if the image $\mathbf{x}_i$ is labeled as relevant, $y_i = -1$ if the image $\mathbf{x}_i$ is labeled as irrelevant. The classification function becomes then a relevance function whose value reflects the relevance of unlabeled data with respect to their similarity to the query.

Active learning strategies [103] aim at minimizing classification error over the whole set of images $\mathcal{B}$ by selecting elements from the unlabeled data pool $\mathcal{U}$ in $\mathcal{B}$ which are the most "informative" and thus should be annotated to improve the most the classification. This specific process, compared to simple classification methods, is called *sampling strategy* in [37]. The user, considered as an expert, must then iteratively annotate as positive (relevant) or negative (irrelevant) strategically selected images [98], in a process called *relevance feedback loop* [181, 233].

Such strategies are particularly relevant in image interactive learning context since only few annotations should be required from the user to define the training set. As a consequence the training set is small, new annotated data must thus provide highest classification improvements.

The user considered as an expert providing annotations to the system can then be represented by a function $s : \mathcal{B} \rightarrow \{-1, 1\}$, which assigns a label to an image of the database. The crucial point is now to define the criterion whose minimum will provide the example leading to an optimum with respect to the objective.

In classification context, the criterion to be minimized is commonly the classification error on unlabeled dataset $\mathcal{U}$, over all the classification functions f_A. In the case where only one image $\mathbf{x}_i$ has to be selected, this minimization is computed over all f_A on the previous training set A augmented with the annotation $s(\mathbf{x}_i)$ of the image $\mathbf{x}_i$:

$$i^* = \underset{\mathbf{x}_i \in \mathcal{U}}{\arg\min} R(f_{A \cup \{(\mathbf{x}_i, s(\mathbf{x}_i))\}}) \tag{3.30}$$

with $R(f_A)$ a risk function, which can have different definitions depending on the approximation introduced in its evaluation:

- For instance, Roy & Mc Callum [179] propose a technique to determine the data $\mathbf{x}_i$ which, once added to the training set A with user annotation $s(\mathbf{x}_i)$, minimizes the error of generalization. This problem cannot be directly solved, since the user annotation $s(\mathbf{x}_i)$ of each $\mathbf{x}_i$ image is unknown. Roy & Mc Callum [179] thus propose to approximate the risk function $R(f_A)$ for both possible annotations, positive and negative. The labels $s(\mathbf{x}_i)$, being unknown on $\mathcal{U}$, are estimated by training 2 classifiers for both possible labels on each unlabeled data $\mathbf{x}_i$.
- Another selection strategy has been proposed by Tong et al. [207]. Their SVM_{active} method aims at focusing on the most uncertain data $\mathbf{x}$: $f_A(\mathbf{x}) \sim 0$. The solution to the minimization problem in eq. (3.30) is then:

$$i^* = \underset{\mathbf{x}_i \in \mathcal{U}}{\arg\min} (|f_A(\mathbf{x}_i)|) \tag{3.31}$$

- In [31], Brinker incorporates a diversity metric into sample selection that outperforms previous methods. This method is named *angle diversity* and represents now, for sample selection, the state of the art. The main idea is to select the image that is the most uncertain while at the same time is the less similar to already labeled images A. The solution to the minimization problem in eq. (3.30) is rewritten:

$$i^* = \underset{\mathbf{x}_i \in \mathcal{U}}{\arg\min} (\lambda * |f_A(\mathbf{x}_i)| + (1 - \lambda)(\underset{\mathbf{x}_j \in A}{\max} \frac{|K(\mathbf{x}_i, \mathbf{x}_j)|}{\sqrt{K(\mathbf{x}_i, \mathbf{x}_i)K(\mathbf{x}_j, \mathbf{x}_j)}})) \tag{3.32}$$

λ is a parameter which allows to balance the diversity and the uncertainty.

For all these methods, once the image $\mathbf{x}_{i^*}$ is labeled, this image is added to the training set A. The classifier is then retrained to update the relevance function f_A. However, one of the main drawbacks of all these methods is that to find the optimal image the whole database must be ranked with respect to f_A output, after each interactive labeling iteration.

In a Content-Based Information Retrieval context, a dedicated criterion may lead to improved results (regarding the objective): Gosselin et al. [82] proposed to maximize a Mean Average Precision (MAP) criterion instead of a classification error in order to better fit to CBIR objective.

3.3 Conclusion

In this chapter, starting from the set of visual local descriptors described in Chapter 2, the so-called Bag-of-Features, the main stages for image representation, comparison and classification have been introduced.

We have detailed the standard processing pipeline for image representation following two steps: (i) feature coding, and (ii) pooling in order to get the image descriptor. These two steps are the most widespread technique to easily design a similarity measure on Bags-of-Features by transforming BoFs into one vector and considering then any similarity function on vectors. Clustering the feature space provide a codebook on which first all the local descriptors are projected to in order to *code* the feature distribution. The spatial aggregation of the projected codes during the pooling step provide then some invariance.

We have further extensively described alternative strategies to preserve more information by accounting for all local feature matching into the similarity measures. If among these techniques, the voting strategy met a high success for copy detection context, we have focused on presenting more semantic-oriented matching between complex data structures. Indeed, Bags-of-Features belonging to sets of subsets of the feature space which is not a vector space, require powerful similarity functions. The kernel functions defining similarity between data from non-metric spaces, even from non-vector spaces, have thus attracted lots of efforts and we have presented here two powerful kernel dealing accounting for feature spatial information. The main advantage of kernel functions is their intrinsic embeddability into most efficient machine learning algorithms.

We have focused in the last part on SVM and Boosting which have been very successful for the last decade, in various research and engineering areas, from text categorization to image recognition. We have presented not only these two frameworks in detail but also new trends in machine learning as Multiple Kernel Learning in both SVM and Boosting contexts and as active learning strategies.

Chapter 4
Spatial and multi-resolution context in visual indexing

Jenny Benois-Pineau, Aurélie Bugeau, Svebor Karaman, Rémi Mégret

Abstract Recent trends in visual indexing make appear a large family of methods which use a local image representation via descriptors associated to the interest points, see chapter 2. Such approaches mostly "forget" any structure in the image considering unordered sets of descriptors or their histograms as image model. Hence, more advanced approaches try to overcome this drawback by adding spatial arrangements to the interest points. In this chapter we will present two trends in incorporation of spatial context into visual description, such as considering spatial context in the process of matching of signatures on one hand and design of structural descriptors which are then used in a global Bag-of-Visual-Words (BoVW) approach on the other hand. As images and video are mainly available in a compressed form, we shortly review global descriptors extracted from compressed stream and hence less sensible to compression artifacts. Furthermore, on the basis of scalable, multi-resolution/multi-scale visual content representation in modern compression standards, we study how this multi-resolution context can be efficiently incorporated into a BoVW approach.

4.1 Introduction

If one can try today to trace the origins of approaches for indexing and retrieval of visual information such as images, videos and visual objects in them, tree main sources could be identified. They are i) text indexing and retrieval approaches, ii) visual coding by vector quantization, iii) structural pattern recognition.

The first two families of methods together with local image analysis inspired the Bag-of-Visual-Words (BoVW) approach which has been exhaustively presented in chapters 2 and 3. In this approach the visual content of an image, a video frame or an object of interest is characterized by a global signature. The latter represent histograms of quantized visual descriptors obtained by the analysis of local neighbourhoods. Hence the spatial relations in image plane between regions in images and object parts are lost.

Conversely, spatial relations are at the core of structural pattern recognition, where spatial graph models are used to describe the visual content. In this case the nodes of the graph represent the visual primitives extracted from the images during an analysis step, and encode elements such as homogeneous regions, linear primitives from contour and skeleton or points of interest. The graph edges encode the spatial relations of the primitives in the image plane. Hence matching and similarity search between visual entities can be formulated as a graph-matching problem [195, 177].

In the case of large graphs covering the whole image content the graph matching becomes computationnaly heavy and cannot be deployed at a large scale for visual indexing and retrieval. Therefore, given the need of analysis of video content practically "on-the-fly" in broadcast applications, the tremendous volumes of visual information in image and video databases make classical methods of structural pattern recognition inapplicable.

Hence, spatial context has been incorporated in visual indexing approaches by relating visual signatures to more local areas in image plane, and matching characteristic points for similarity refining, etc. Furthermore, for the sake of scalability, it is very much seducing to incorporate multi-resolution and multi-scale representation of visual content in image and video retrieval in order to realise a "progressive" indexing and retrieval which allows to fasten the search operation. Indeed, to recognise a visual scene, humans hardly need any fine details available at full resolution, but successfully fulfil the visual recognition task on under-scaled and degraded versions of the content. This was the subject of "Rough indexing" paradigm we developed for indexing and retrieval of HD video [139]. The incorporation of a multi-resolution representation not only at the level of images, but also at the level of salient region extraction (SIFT) or characteristic points, seems also a promising way in visual indexing.

Nevertheless all these approaches comprise the same fundamental step which consists in detecting features in the raw image domain. With regard to the properties of visual content to analyse this detection may be unstable. Indeed, image and video content items are stored in repositories and exchanged via heterogeneous channels of visual information in a compressed form. They are practically never available in a raw pixel domain. Yet image and video compression artefacts affect interest point detectors or other differential features. On the other hand, modern compression standards such as JPEG2000 [2] already incorporate multi-resolution/multi-scale representations.

Hence in this chapter we are interested in these two aspects: incorporation of spatial context in visual content indexing and retrieval and multi-resolution/multi-scale content description. In section 4.2 we will review methods which incorporate spatial context into indexing and retrieval of visual content and present our recent works on the border of BoVW and structural pattern recognition approaches we call "GraphWords". In section 4.3 we are interested in multi-resolution/multi-scale strategies and, in the follow up of our research under the Rough Indexing paradigm, propose visual indexing approaches based on the wavelet pyramids of the JPEG2000 standard. The conclusions and perspectives are drawn in section 4.4

4.2 Incorporating spatial context

The standard Bag-of-Visual-Words approach, presented in chapter 3, represents an image by a global histogram of visual words distribution. This representation does not cover one important part of an image or an object: the spatial organization.

In the past few years, several methods have tried to overcome the lack of spatial information and relations between interest regions in the BoVW framework. For example, a method for integrating the spatial information was presented in [166], where after applying a BoVW approach for retrieval the top ranked images where re-ranked by applying a LO-RANSAC [45] algorithm with affine transformations. This method can be seen as a post-processing. We will focus in this section on methods where the spatial organization is fully integrated in the approaches.

We will first report approaches that use local histograms instead of global histograms. Then we review approaches which introduce spatial context during the matching process. Structural pattern have been widely represented by graphs, we will show that graph matching is an efficient approach for object recognition but can hardly be applied to large databases retrieval. Finally we will introduce our research which tries to overcome the ambiguity of the visual words relying on very local features and the lack of spatial organization in the BoVW framework.

4.2.1 Local histograms of visual words

One popular and successful approach to overcome the lack of spatial information within the BoVW framework is the Spatial Pyramid Matching Kernel (SPMK) approach introduced in [126] and referenced in chapter 3 . The method uses the Pyramid Match Kernel [86] in order to compare image signatures according to a visual vocabulary but applying the pyramid construction to the coordinates of the features in the image space.

The image plane is successively partitioned into blocks according to the "levels" of pyramid. At level $l = 0$ the only block is the whole image. At all other levels up to $l = L$ the image is partitioned into $2^l x 2^l$ blocks. The features are quantized into K discrete classes according to a visual vocabulary C obtained by traditional clustering techniques in feature space. Only features of the same class k can be matched. For a pair of images X and Y to compare, each class k gives two sets of two-dimensional vectors, X_k and Y_k, representing the coordinates of features of class k found in images X and Y respectively. Let us denote $H^l(X_k)$ the histogram of features of class k in image X according to the fixed partitioning of the pyramid at level l. Using the histogram intersection similarity measure $\mathcal{I}$ introduced in chapter 3, the SPMK for features of class k is defined as:

$$K^L(X_k, Y_k) = \frac{1}{2^L}\mathcal{I}(H^0(X_k), H^0(Y_k)) + \sum_{l=1}^{L} \frac{1}{2^{L-l+1}}\mathcal{I}(H^l(X_k), H^l(Y_k)) \qquad (4.1)$$

The final kernel (4.2) is the sum of the kernels associated to each feature class:

$$K^L(X, Y) = \sum_{k=1}^{K} K^L(X_k, Y_k) \qquad (4.2)$$

For $L = 0$ the approach reduces to a standard BoVW.

Experiments on three publicly available image databases show significant improvements using the Spatial Pyramid Matching approach compared to BoVW. However, since locations are expressed in absolute coordinates, the representation is unsuitable in the case of spatial displacement of the object of interest unless exhaustive search is done using a spatial sub-window.

In [6], Albatal et al. note two important limitations of the BoVW framework as visual words are much more ambiguous than text words and that in the global histogram representation, all information related to topological organization of the regions of interest in the image is lost. They have proposed a method to create groups of regions in the image to form areas which are spatially larger than the individual regions and have the same robust visual properties. As shown in [231], grouping several regions is more discriminative for object classification than individual regions.

Albatal et al. uses a "Single Link" clustering function, with a topological proximity criterion based on the Euclidean distance between the regions of interest. This criterion defines two regions as close if the Euclidean distance between their centres is less or equal than the sum of their radii. This type of clustering does not depend on the starting point and ensure that the created groups are disjoint. Each cluster corresponds to a set of regions that defines a "visual phrase".

Each Visual Phrase is then represented as a BoVW with regard to a visual dictionary C. By construction, resulting visual phrases are invariant to scale, rotation, and translation transformations and to brightness changes.

The approach is evaluated on an automatic annotation task on the VOC2009 collection. The evaluation shows that using Visual Phrases only yields poorer results than the baseline (BoVW on the whole images). According to the authors this is mainly because Visual Phrases account only for the description of the objects while the baseline approach integrates information about the background as well. A late fusion of recognition score for each image enhances the performance above baseline's initial results. This approach builds local BoVWs but does not take into account the spatial organization for description of the visual phrases.

4.2.2 Context-matching kernels

The previous approaches have defined local histograms by a fixed partitioning or data adaptive partitioning. However, they still miss description of spatial configuration of features.

A spatial weighting approach was introduced in [140] for object recognition on cluttered background. The hypothetical object mask is estimated in test images by matching quantized features with those in training images. During the matching affine transformations are applied accordingly to the scale and orientation of feature points. The final hypothesis segmentation mask is a weighted sum of the transformed masks. The test features are then weighted according to this mask thus giving lower weights to background features.

In [183] and [182], Sahbi et al. have introduced a kernel which takes into account both feature similarity "alignment quality" and spatial alignment in a "neighbourhood" criteria. Let us denote two sets of interest regions $S_A = \{r_1^A, \ldots, r_n^A\}$ and $S_B = \{r_1^B, \ldots, r_m^B\}$ extracted from two images A and B respectively, where a region r_i^I of image I is defined by its coordinates (x_i^I, y_i^I) and a feature f_i^I: $r_i^I = (x_i^I, y_i^I, f_i^I)$. Considering any pair of regions (r_i^I, r_j^J) of two images I and J, let us denote D the matrix of dissimilarity in the feature space: $D_{r_i^I, r_j^J} = d(r_i^I, r_j^J) = \left\| f_i^I - f_j^J \right\|_2$. Let $\mathcal{N}(r_i^I)$ be the set of neighbours of r_i^I. Let us denote P the proximity matrix defined according to the neighbourhood criterion:

$$P_{r_i^I, r_j^J} = \begin{cases} 1 & \text{if } I = J \text{ and } r_j^J \in \mathcal{N}(r_i^I) \\ 0 & \text{otherwise} \end{cases} \tag{4.3}$$

The Context-Dependent Kernel K is the unique solution of the energy function minimization problem and is the limit of $K^{(t)}$ defined according to the following equations:

$$K^{(t)} = \frac{G(K^{(t-1)})}{\left\| G(K^{(t-1)}) \right\|_1} \tag{4.4}$$

$$G(K) = exp(-\frac{D}{\beta} + \frac{\alpha}{\beta} P K^{(t-1)} P)$$

$$K^{(0)} = \frac{exp(\frac{-D}{\beta})}{\left\| exp(\frac{-D}{\beta}) \right\|_1}$$

Where exp represents the coefficient-wise exponential and $\|M\|_1 = \sum_{ij} |M_{ij}|$ represents the L_1 matrix norm. The two parameters β and α can be seen respectively as weights for features distance and spatial consistency propagation. The CDK convergence is fast, in [182] only one iteration was applied. Then the authors use the kernel values thus obtained for classification with SVM. The CDK was evaluated on the Olivetti face database, the Smithsonian leaf set, the MNIST digit database and ImageClef@ICPR set showing significant improvements of equal error rate (ERR) compared to Context-Free Kernels.

4.2.3 Graph-matching

At the other end of the spectrum of methods addressing the problem of object recognition, the spatial information has often been incorporated through a graph representation. The most common idea is to build a graph model of an object, the recognition process consisting in matching the prototype to a candidate one.

In [177], a pseudo-hierarchical graph matching has been introduced. Using local interest points, the pseudo-hierarchical aspect relies on progressively incorporating "smaller" model features (in terms of scale) as the hierarchy increases. The edges of the graph were defined accordingly to a scale-normalized proximity criterion. The model graph is matched to a new scene by a relaxation process starting from a graph model including only points of highest scale and adding smaller model features during the matching process. In [128], the graph model was defined according to locally affine-invariant geometric constraint. Each point is represented as an affine combination of its neighboring points. Defining an objective function taking into account both feature and geometric matching costs, the matching is solved by linear programming. These approaches are efficient for object matching, however when dealing with a large amount of image candidates, the matching process becomes too costly.

The comparison of graphs can be also expressed under the form of graph kernels [220], that allows to consider graphs as belonging to a RKHS, and apply standard tools such as SVM classifiers. In particular, random walk kernels are defined by considering a simultaneous walk on the two graphs to compare, with corresponds to a random walk on their direct product. Other approach transforms a graph into a set of paths [204], and apply a minor kernel to the obtained set of simpler features. Such measures rely on the extraction of meaningful sets of features, or on the exhaustive evaluation of edge matching possibilities, which scales at least quadratically with the number of node of the graphs, or requires a very sparse structures, thus limiting the size of the considered graphs in practice.

Based on the previous discussion, we believe that integrating spatial information with local interest points into a BoVW can be an elegant approach to overcome the limitations of both the BoVW framework and object matching in the case of large scale retrieval. Therefore, we will present a new semi-structural approach for content description, by a "Bag-of-Graph-Words", and study its application to object recognition.

4.2.4 Graph Words

The idea of the method consists in describing image content by a set of "small" graphs with good properties of invariance and then in fitting these features to a BoVW approach. Hence the spatial context is taken into account at the feature level.

Another property we seek is a structural multi-resolution: the graphs will be of increasing size with a nested topology of nodes.

Graph feature construction

Let us consider a graph $G = (X,E)$ where X is a set of nodes corresponding to some feature points $x_{k,k=1,..,K}$, in image plane (we take SURF points) and $E = \{e_{kl}\}_{k=1,..,K,l=1,..,K}$ is a set of edges $e_{kl} = (x_k, x_l)$ connecting these points. We call such a graph a "graph feature". We will build these features upon sets of neighbouring feature points in image plane. In order to build such graphs two questions have to be addressed:

- the choice of a feature point set X;
- the design of the connectivity edges E.

To define the feature point sets X we first select the "seeds". Around them, other feature points will be selected to build each graph feature. Selected seeds have to form a set of SURF points which are more likely to be detected in various instances of the same object. SURF points are detected where local maxima of the response of the approximated Hessian determinant are reached [16]. The points with higher response correspond to more salient visual structures and are therefore more likely to be repeatable. Hence, we select them as seeds. Considering a fixed number of seeds N_{Seeds}, we can define the set of seeds $S = \{s_1, \ldots, s_{N_{Seeds}}\}$.

Given S, our aim is to add partial structural information of the object while keeping the discriminative power of SURF key points. We will therefore define graphs over the seeds and their neighboring SURF points. Finding the k spatial nearest SURF neighbors of each seed s_i defines the set of neighbors $P_i = \{p_1, \ldots, p_k\}$.

Hence the set of nodes X^{G_i} for each graph G_i is defined as the seed s_i and the neighbours P_i. For the edges we use the Delaunay triangulation [198] of the set $\{s_i\} \cup P_i$, which is invariant with regard to affine transformations of image plane preserving angles: translation, rotation and scaling.

The nested layered approach

The choice of the number of nodes in a graph feature obviously depends on various factors such as image resolution, complexity of visual scene or its sharpness... This choice is difficult a priori. Instead we propose a hierarchy of "nested" graphs for the same image, capturing structural information of increasingly higher order and illustrate it in Figure 4.1. Let us introduce a set of L "layers". We say that the graph G_i^l at layer l and the graph G_i^{l+1} at layer $l + 1$ are nested if the set of nodes of graph G_i^l is included in the set of nodes of graph G_i^{l+1}: $X_i^l \subset X_i^{l+1}$. Note that, so defined, the number of graphs at each layer is the same. Furthermore, in the definition (by construction) of graph features a node can belong to more than one graph of the same layer. We still consider these graph features as separate graphs.

Fig. 4.1 The nested approach. Bottom to top: SURF seed depicted as the white node, 3 neighbours graph where neighbours are in black, 6 neighbours graph and 9 neighbours graph at the top level.

Introducing this layered approach, where each layer adds more structural information, we can define graphs of increasing size when moving from one layer to the next one. Each layer has its own set of neighbours around each seed s_i and the Delaunay triangulation is performed on each layer separately. To avoid a large number of layers, the number of nodes added at each layer should induce a significant change of structural information. To build a Delaunay triangulation, at least two points have to be added to a single seed. Adding one more node may yield three triangles instead of just one, resulting in a more complete local pattern. Therefore, the number of nodes added from one layer to the upper one is fixed to three. We define four layers, the bottom one containing only one SURF point, the seed, and the top one containing a graph built upon the seed and its 9 nearest neighbours.

Graph comparison

In order to integrate these new graph features in a BoVW framework a dissimilarity measure and a clustering method have to be defined. In this section, we define the dissimilarity measure. We are dealing with attributed graphs, where nodes can be compared with respect to their visual appearance. Although it could be possible to take into account similarities of node features only or the topology of the graph only, more information can be obtained by combining both for defining a dissimilarity measure between local graphs. To achieve this we will investigate the use of the Context Dependent Kernel (CDK), see 4.2.2.

The definition of the CDK relies on two matrices: D which contains the distances between node features, and T which contains the topology of the graphs being compared. Considering two graphs A and B with respective number of nodes m and n, let us denote C the union of the two graphs:

$$C = A \oplus B$$

$$\text{with } \begin{cases} x_i^C = x_i^A & \text{for } i \in [1..m] = I_A \\ x_i^C = x_{i-m}^B & \text{for } i \in [m+1..m+n] = I_B \end{cases} \tag{4.5}$$

with I_A and I_B, the sets of indices of each graph nodes.

The feature correspondence square matrix D of size $(m+n) \times (m+n)$ contains the "entry-wise" L2-norm of the difference between SURF features:

$$D = (d_{ij}) \text{ where } d_{ij} = \left\| x_i^C - x_j^C \right\|_2 \tag{4.6}$$

The square topology matrix T (corresponding to the proximity matrix P in 4.2.2) of size $(m+n) \times (m+n)$ defines the connectivity between two vertices x_i^C and x_j^C. In this work we define a crisp connectivity as we set T_{ij} to one if an edge connects the vertices x_i^C and x_j^C and 0 otherwise. Hence, only sub matrices with both lines and columns in I_A or I_B are not entirely null. More precisely, we can define sub matrices T_{AA} and T_{BB} corresponding to the topology of each graph A and B respectively, while sub matrices T_{AB} and T_{BA} are entirely null, vertices of graphs A and B are not connected.

$$T = (T_{ij}) \text{ where } T_{ij} = \begin{cases} 1 & \text{if edge } (x_i^C, x_j^C) \text{ belongs to A or B} \\ 0 & \text{otherwise} \end{cases} \tag{4.7}$$

The CDK denoted K is computed by an iterative process consisting of the propagation of the similarity in the description space according to the topology matrix as detailed in 4.2.2.

Similarly to the definition of sub matrices in topology matrix T we can define sub matrices in the kernel matrix K. The sub matrix $K_{AB}^{(t)}$ represents the strength of the inter-graph links between graphs A and B once the topology has been taken into account. We can therefore define a kernel-wise similarity γ between graphs A and B as:

$$\gamma(A,B) = \sum_{\{i \in I_A, j \in I_b\}} K_{ij}^{(t)} \in [0,1] \tag{4.8}$$

and induce the dissimilarity as standard kernel distance [188] by evaluating the sum of self-similarity measures of graphs A and B minus twice the cross-similarity between graphs:

$$\rho(A,B) = \gamma(A,A) + \gamma(B,B) - 2\gamma(A,B) \in [0,1] \tag{4.9}$$

This dissimilarity measure will be applied separately on each layer. However, for the bottom layer, since there is no topology to take into account for isolated points we will use directly the "entrywise" L2-norm (4.6). This corresponds to an approximation of the dissimilarity measure used for graphs features by considering a graph with a single point.

Visual dictionaries and signatures

The state-of-the-art approach for computing the visual dictionary C of a set of features is the use of the K-means clustering algorithm [201] with a large number of clusters, often several thousands, where the code-word is usually the center of a cluster. This approach is not suitable for the graph-features because using the K means clustering algorithm implies iteratively moving the cluster centers with interpolation. Therefore, we use a hierarchical agglomerative (HAG) clustering [190] which does not require graph-interpolation. The median graph G of each cluster V, defined as $median = \underset{G \in V}{argmin} \sum_{i=1}^{m} \|v_i - G\|$, i.e. the graph minimizing the distance to all the graphs v_i of cluster V, represents a code-word.

When targeting object classification on a large database, it can be interesting to use a two pass clustering approach as proposed in [84], as it enables a gain in terms of computational cost. Here, the first pass of the HAG clustering will be run on all the features extracted from training images of one object. The second pass is applied on the centers of clusters generated by the first pass on all objects of the database.

Finally, the usual representation of an image in a BoVW with the dictionary C is built. The BoVW are normalized to sum to one by dividing each value by the number of features extracted from the image. The distance between two images is defined as the L_1 distance between BoVWs (as defined in chapter 3).

Experiments

The approach is evaluated on publicly available data sets in the problem of object retrieval. The choice of the data sets are guided by the need of annotated objects. We thus chose two datasets.

The SIVAL (Spatially Independent, Variable Area, and Lighting) data set [173] includes 25 objects, each of them being present in 60 images taken in 10 various environment and different poses yielding a total of 1500 images. This data set is quite challenging as the objects are depicted in various lighting conditions and poses. The second one is the well known Caltech-101 [67] data set, composed of 101 object categories. The categories are different types of animals, plants or objects. A snippet of both data sets is shown in Figure 4.2.

Evaluation protocol

We separate learning and testing images by a random selection. On each data set, 30 images of each category are selected as learning images for building the visual

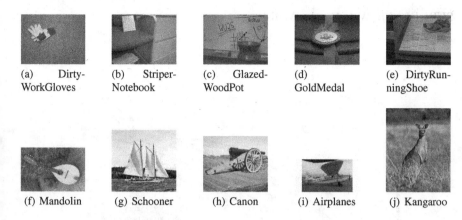

(a) Dirty-WorkGloves   (b) Striper-Notebook   (c) Glazed-WoodPot   (d) GoldMedal   (e) DirtyRun-ningShoe

(f) Mandolin   (g) Schooner   (h) Canon   (i) Airplanes   (j) Kangaroo

Fig. 4.2 Excerpts from image data sets. SIVAL (a)-(e), Caltech-101 (f)-(j)

dictionaries and for the retrieval task. Some categories of Caltech-101 have several hundred of images when others have only a few. The testing images are therefore a random selection of the remaining images up to 50. The first pass clustering yields 500 clusters from all the features of all learning images of each object. The final dictionary size varies in the range 50-5000. Details on the experimental setup can be found in [117]. Each layer of graph-features will yield its own dictionary. We compare our method with standard BoVW approach. For that purpose, we use all the SURF features available on all images of the learning database to build the BoVW dictionary by k-means clustering.

The graph features are built only on a selected subset of all SURF points detected in an image. To analyse the influence of this selection, signatures are computed for the set of SURF which have been selected to build the different layers of graphs. These configurations will be referred to as SURF3NN, SURF6NN and SURF9NN corresponding respectively to all the points upon which graphs with 3, 6 and 9 nearest neighbours have been defined.

For each query image and each database image, the signatures are computed for isolated SURF and the different layers of graphs. We have investigated the combination of isolated SURF and the different layers of graphs by an early fusion of signatures i.e. concatenating the BoVWs. For SIVAL this concatenation has been done with the signature from the selected SURF corresponding to the highest level whereas for Caltech-101 we used the classical BoW SURF signature. Finally, the L_1-distance between histograms is computed to compare two images.

The performance is evaluated by the Mean Average Precision (MAP) measure. Here, the average precision metric is evaluated for each test image of an object, and the MAP is the mean of these values for all the images of an object in the test set. For all categories, we measure the performance by the average value of the MAP of objects.

SURF based BoW vs Graphs Words

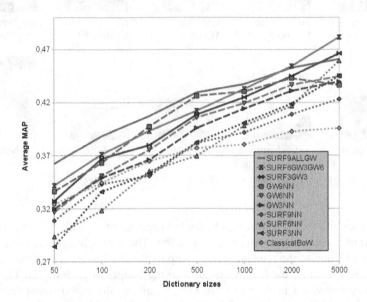

Fig. 4.3 Average MAP on the whole SIVAL data set. Isolated SURF features are the dotted curves, single layer Graphs Words are drawn as dashed curves and the multilayer approach in solid curves.

First of all, it is interesting to analyse if the graph words approach obtains similar performances compared to the classical BoVW approach using only SURF features. This is depicted in Figure 4.3, Figure 4.5 and 4.6 where isolated SURF points are depicted as dotted lines and single layer of graph words are dashed lines. At first glance, we can see that for SIVAL isolated SURF features perform the poorest, separated layers of graphs perform better. Our clustering approach seems to give worse results for very small size of dictionaries but better results for dictionaries larger than 500 visual words, which are the commonly used configurations in BoVW approaches. Each layer of graph words performs much better than the SURF upon which they are built. The introduction of the topology in our features have a significant impact on the recognition performance using the same set of SURF features.

The average performance hides however differences in the performance on some specific objects. To illustrate this we select two object categories where graph features and SURF features give different performances in Figure 4.5 and Figure 4.6. For the object "banana" from SIVAL, the isolated SURF features outperform the graph approach, see Figure 4.5. This can be explained as the "banana" object represents a small part of the bounding box and is poorly textured. In some environments the background is highly textured, this characteristics induce many SURF points detected in it and these SURF points may have a higher response than those detected on the object. This will lead to the construction of many "noisy" graph features on

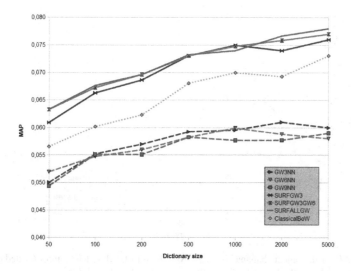

Fig. 4.4 Average MAP on the whole Caltech-101 data set. Isolated SURF features are the dotted curves, single layer Graphs Words are drawn as dashed curves and the multilayer approach in solid curves.

the background and less on the object. On the other hand, for the "Faces" category from Caltech-101 the graph features perform better, see Figure 4.6. Here, the object covers most of the bounding box and many SURF points are detected. In this situation, the graph features capture a larger part of the object than isolated SURF points, making them more discriminative.

This unequal discriminative power of each layer leads naturally to the use of the combination of the different layers in a single visual signature.

The multilayer approach

The combination of graphs and SURF features upon which the graphs have been built is done by the concatenation of the signatures of each layer. The three curves in solid lines in Figure 4.3 correspond to the multilayer approach using only the two bottom layers (SURF + 3 nearest neighbours graphs) depicted with double "horizontal" triangles, the three bottom layers (SURF + 3 nearest neighbours graphs + 6 nearest neighbours) depicted with double "vertical" triangles and all the layers depicted by a simple poly-line. For SIVAL, the improvement in the average MAP is clear, and each addition of layer improves the results. The average performance of the combination always outperforms the performance of each layer taken separately.

For Caltech-101, see Figure 4.4, the average MAP values of all methods are much lower which is not surprising as there are much more categories and images. Single layer of graphs gives lower results than the classical BoVW framework on SURF features. However, the combination of all layers outperforms here again SURF or

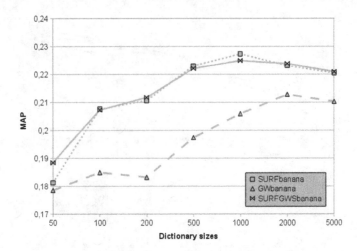

Fig. 4.5 MAP for the object "banana" from SIVAL where isolated SURF features (dotted curves) outperforms graphs (dashed curves). The multilayer approach is the solid curve.

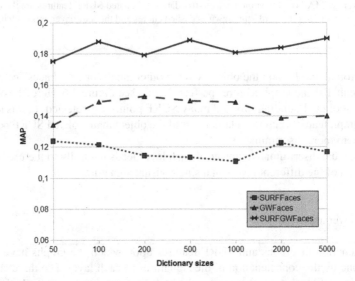

Fig. 4.6 MAP for category "Faces" from Caltech-101 where graphs (dashed curves) outperforms isolated SURF features (dotted curves). The multilayer approach is the solid curves.

graphs used separately. The performance of single layers of graphs can be explained as the fixed number (300) of seeds selection induces for Caltech-101 a strong over-lapping of graphs as the average number of SURF points within the bounding box is much lower than for SIVAL. This may give less discriminant graph words as it will be harder to determine separable clusters in the clustering process.

The detailed results presented in Figure 4.5 and Figure 4.6 show that the com-bination, depicted as a solid line, of the visual signatures computed on each layer separately performs better or at least as well as the best isolated feature.

4.3 Multi-resolution in visual indexing

The images available today on the web are rarely in their raw form as it would re-quire a too huge amount of space to store them. Before being processed, the encoded data is generally decoded. Instead of decoding it completely, some approaches in-tend to take advantage of the data available in the compressed stream with only partial decoding, thus working in the rough indexing paradigm [139]. Modern stan-dards of visual coding are "scalable", which means that in the same code-stream multi-resolution versions of the same content are available. This gives a tremendous opportunity to follow multi-resolution strategy in visual indexing directly using the new low-level features available in code streams. The advantage is obvious. On one hand, the signal will not be deteriorated by double resolution reduction (one when encoding and one when building multi-resolution pyramids on decoded images and videos). On the other hand, computational time savings will be achieved. JPEG2000 standard for images and MJPEG2000 standard for videos have this seducing prop-erty of scalability. In this section, we aim at performing image indexing on images encoded in JPEG2000. Following the line of research on rough indexing paradigm, we propose to make use of the multi-resolution information from the wavelet basis and study different techniques to perform indexing in this context.

4.3.1 Low resolution and Rough Indexing Paradigm

When aiming at multi-resolution indexing of visual content, the natural step is to get robust results on the lowest available resolution. The rough indexing paradigm has been introduced in [139] for foreground object extraction purposes. It enables a fast and approximate analysis of multimedia content at a poor resolution. Indeed, it takes advantages of the content directly available in the compressed streams (*e.g.* DC coefficients, motion vectors from video streams, region-based colour segmenta-tion...). It has been used for different applications in the recent years: shot boundary detection [155], object retrieval [43, 44] or video indexing [149]. More specifically, in [149], the HD video is only partially decoded to perform video indexing after detecting moving objects. A similar methodology is presented in [20]. These methods are all designed for content having the property of scalable representation. In the same line of research, Adami et al. studied a scalable joint data and descriptor encoding of image collections [3]. This work has been extended to videos in [4].

Other works that can be seen as closely related to the rough data processing are those focusing on the analysis of tiny images. Namely, Torralba et al. [208] propose a framework that allows performing object recognition in a huge database (tens of millions images). To that end, they directly process low-resolution 32×32 color images. This low resolution could correspond to the coarsest level of coded images.

In this chapter, we only focus on image indexing and do not address the video indexing problem. The rough data then only consists of partially decoded colour/intensity information.

4.3.2 Multi-resolution and multiscale in image indexing

For raw data the multi-resolution comes from the construction of image pyramids (Gaussian pyramids for instance), whereas for encoded data (such as JPEG2000 images) it is directly available from the wavelet decomposition. As always, these techniques rely on the computation of local or global descriptors on the resulting multi-resolution multi-scale pyramids.

Global descriptors are generally based on computation of histograms. The use of multi-resolution histograms for recognition was first proposed in [90]. The multi-resolution decomposition is computed with Gaussian filtering. A filtered image $I *\mathcal{G}(l)$ is the result of the convolution of the image I with the Gaussian filter:

$$\mathcal{G}(l) = \frac{1}{2\pi l\sigma^2}exp\left(-\frac{x^2+y^2}{2l\sigma^2}\right),$$

where σ is the standard deviation of the filter and l is the resolution.

An example of the use of histograms in the rough indexing paradigm can be found in [149]. This paper addresses the problem of scalable indexing of HD videos encoded in the MJPEG2000 standard. After detecting moving objects, their indexing is performed. A global descriptor is built for the object. It consists of a pair of two histograms:

$$H = \{h_{LL}^k, h_{HF}^k, k = 1\ldots K\},$$

where K is the number of levels in pyramid defined in JPEG2000. The first histogram h_{LL} is the YUV joint histogram of LL coefficients. The second one, h_{HF}, is computed from the High Frequency (*i.e.* HL, LH and HH) sub-band. Each sub-band represents a different orientation: HL horizontal, LH vertical and HH diagonal. The histogram h_{HF} is finally the histogram of mean absolute values of coefficients LH, HL and HH. Hence the invariance to rotation to multiple of 45° is obtained.

Amongst few multi-resolution approaches existing today, the most known is the so-called spatial pyramid matching (SPM) [126], also referenced in chapter 3. BoVW are built on nested partitions of image plane from coarse-to-fine. Nevertheless, this approach cannot be qualified as a truly "multi-resolution", as the features and level image descriptors (sparse SIFT) are built only on the full resolution image. The adaptation of SPM to Gaussian scale space has been proposed in [193]. Spatial pyramids are computed at different scales which allow combining different levels of details.

In our approach, on the contrary, we aim to incorporate multi-scale representation of image content in the whole feature extraction, quantization and matching process.

4.3.3 Multi-resolution features and visual dictionaries

Based on the rationale we expressed before we present and analyze some approaches for indexing images encoded in JPEG2000 using its "natural" multi-scale representation of visual content. From the Daubechies pyramid, we only use the LL sub-band at all decomposition levels. All the methods described could also directly be used on uncompressed data by computing a multi-resolution pyramid by standard Gaussian filtering and sub-sampling. Here, we focus only on methods inspired from the BoVW and the SPM approaches.

Multi-resolution approach on wavelet pyramids

From the colour Daubechies 9/7 pyramid as defined in JPEG2000, we extract only the Y component of the LL sub-band at $K = 3$ levels of the pyramid. In the following, we denote the different levels of pyramid by k, $k = 1 \ldots K$.

Our approach follows the BoVW scheme with

- level features which are SURF points and descriptors extracted at each level Y_{LL}^k in the wavelet pyramid. We denote a set of features at level k by $\mathcal{D}^k$.
- visual dictionaries we build per level, denoted by C^k, and for all levels together denoted by C. The number of visual words varies from 50 to 5000. Every visual dictionary we refer to is constructed by applying the k-means++ algorithm [8] on the training set (see section 4.3 for more details on training sets).
- image signature which is a histogram of visual words from C^k, denoted by H^k, and built for Y_{LL}^k or a histogram H built for all levels together Y_{LL}^k, $k = 1 \ldots K$ with the global dictionary C.

Hence, the descriptor of an image is the histogram of visual words from appropriate dictionary. To compare the images at different resolution levels in wavelet domain, we use the histogram intersection kernel as a similarity measure. For the BoVWs of two images at level k, this function is given by:

$$\mathcal{I}(H_1^k, H_2^k) = \sum_{i=1}^{N} \min(H_1^k(i), H_2^k(i)). \tag{4.10}$$

N being the number of visual words (vocabulary size).

The proposed description schemes are used for image retrieval and classification. For the simple retrieval scenario, images are ranked according to histogram intersection similarity (4.10) with regard to a query image. The mean average precision is then computed to evaluate the methods. Classification of images is performed with a supervised learning framework with multi-class support vector machine (SVM) using the libSVM library [36] and a *one versus all* rule. For each scheme, a kernel inspired by the pyramid match kernel [86] is provided to the SVM.

As in previous section, all the results presented here are on the two datasets: Caltech-101 and SIVAL. The SURF features are only extracted in a bounding box around the object of interest. The coordinates of the bounding box can be downloaded together with the set of images. The mean average precisions and classification rates on both datasets and for all the methods we present here are presented in Table 4.1, 4.3 and 4.2, 4.4 respectively.

Merging the information at different resolutions

The direct application of BoVW in the context of the rough indexing paradigm consists in applying the BoVW method at the coarsest level ($k = K$) of the wavelet pyramid. Nevertheless the image of low frequency coefficients at this level, Y_{LL}^K, is obviously very blurry and does not contain many interest points. Many important details are lost. The induced visual dictionary C^K and the corresponding signatures H^K are therefore not enough informative. We have tested the application of BoVW at each level independently. The results are visible in the second, third and fourth columns of the four tables at the end of this section. At the finest scale ($k = 1$) it corresponds to applying the BoVW method to the original full-resolution gray-scale image. The classification rates in Table 4.2 and 4.4 come from the following kernel:

$$\kappa_{BoVW}^k(X,Y) = \mathcal{I}(H_X^k, H_Y^k). \tag{4.11}$$

These results permit to confirm that working at the finest scale is more efficient than working at coarsest scales. In particular the number of relevant documents retrieved significantly decreases when using only the information at level $k = 3$. When looking more into details at the precision values, we observed that for some images, processing the coarsest level could improve the results. For instance, for the class *inline_skate* of Caltech 101 the map is 0.09 at level $k = 3$ against 0.02 at level $k = 1$. Similarly for the class *woodrollingpin* of SIVAL, the map is 0.19 at level $k = 3$ against 0.13 at level $k = 1$. Examples of images for which the same conclusion can be drawn are presented in Figure 4.7. A natural extension of mono-level approach is to try to combine information from different levels of a multi-resolution pyramid in the same way we combine structural graph words in the the "early fusion" manner.

Our first attempt has then been to concatenate the histograms at different resolutions H^k, $k = 1 \dots K$ into a unique signature, $\tilde{H}$:

$$\tilde{H} = \cup_{k=1\dots K} H^k.$$

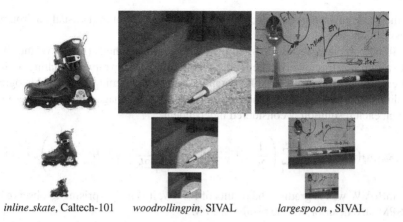

inline_skate, Caltech-101   woodrollingpin, SIVAL   largespoon, SIVAL

Fig. 4.7 Images leading to better results for BoVW at coasest scales. First row: One image from each class at level $k = 1$. Second row: level $k = 2$. Third row: level $k = 3$.

The dimensionality of this vector is $(K.N)$. The same importance is given to all the resolutions so that the concatenation is not weighted. As a reference to BoVW method, we will now refer to this approach as mBoVW (multi-resolution BoVW). The kernel used for classification is given by:

$$\kappa_{mBoVW}(X,Y) = \sum_{k=1}^{K} \mathcal{I}(H_X^k, H_Y^k) = \mathcal{I}(\tilde{H}_X, \tilde{H}_Y). \tag{4.12}$$

It is worth mentioning that this kernel is not related to the pyramid match kernel [86]. Indeed, at each multi-resolution level, the dictionary is different. Results of this method are presented in the sixth column of the different tables. It can be seen that, even if we can find several classes for which it does improve the results compared to the BoVW at level $k = 1$, it globally deteriorates the classification rates and the mean average precision for both databases.

A comparison to SPM [126] is provided in the fifth column. This method has been implemented with three scales (spatial resolution), $L = 3$: 21 histograms, $\mathcal{H}^l$, $l = 0 \ldots \sum_{l=0}^{L-1} 4^l$ are representing each image. The kernel is:

$$\kappa_{SPM}(X,Y) = \sum_{i=1}^{N} \left(\frac{1}{2^L} \mathcal{I}(\mathcal{H}_{X_i}^0, \mathcal{H}_{Y_i}^0) + \sum_{l=1}^{L-1} \frac{1}{2^{L-l+1}} \mathcal{I}(\mathcal{H}_{X_i}^l, \mathcal{H}_{Y_i}^l) \right). \tag{4.13}$$

The application of SPM to the two datasets we are studying lead to opposite conclusions. While it deteriorates the result on the SIVAL database, compared to the standard BoVW at level $k = 1$, an improvement appears on Caltech-101. The main reason for this is that the different objects of SIVAL have been acquired with the same background. It means that SPM is not the best choice to differentiate objects in the same environment, especially when an object is not in its usual environment (loss of context).

To be complete we also merged the two previous methods (mBoVW and SPM) into a common framework called multi-resolution spatial pyramid matching (mSPM). At each resolution of the wavelet pyramid, a spatial pyramid is built. K histograms of dimension $(N\sum_{l=0}^{L-1} 4^l)$ are indeed computed for each image (see figure 4.8). Once again, each resolution is considered independent:

$$\kappa_{mSPM}(X,Y) = \sum_{k=1}^{K}\sum_{i=1}^{N}\left(\frac{1}{2^L}\mathcal{I}(H_{X_i}^{0,k},H_{Y_i}^{0,k}) + \sum_{l=1}^{L-1}\frac{1}{2^{L-l+1}}\mathcal{I}(H_{X_i}^{l,k},H_{Y_i}^{l,k})\right).\qquad(4.14)$$

As mBoVW was degrading the results of BoVW, it is not surprising to observe that mSPM also deteriorates the results of SPM.

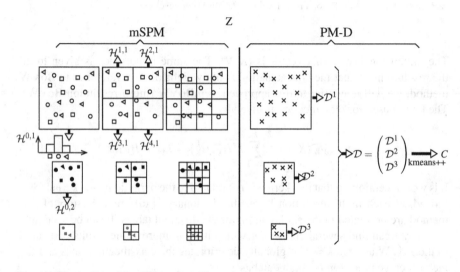

Fig. 4.8 Illustration of the different multi-resolution methods.

Adding the multi-resolution by early fusion of BoVW histograms from each level k is not optimal. Therefore, we elaborated a different strategy for merging the information at different resolutions. Until now, each level k was assigned one dictionary C^k. Here we propose to consider one dictionnary C that is common to all levels. It is computed by using all sets of descriptors $\{\mathcal{D}^k\}_{k=1...K}$. By taking into account all the descriptors at all levels together a more complete vocabulary can be obtained. For each image, the set of all available features is considered: $\mathcal{D} = \cup_{k=1...K}\mathcal{D}^k$. The unique dictionary C is then obtained by clustering this unique set. Each image is finally represented by a unique signature H that incorporates directly the information from all levels. We call this approach Pyramid Matching with Descriptors (PM-D).

The kernel is the same as the one used for the classical BoVW method (equation (4.11)).

Its extension to spatial pyramid matching (SPM-D) is also shown in the tables. In this case, the position of the points at coarsest levels are projected to the finest level before partitioning the space. The results obtained using the combination of the descriptors with these two last methods (PM-D and SPM-D) are the most promising ones on both datasets.

N	BoVW k=0	BoVW k=1	BoVW k=2	SPM [126]	mBoVW	mSPM	SPM-D	PM-D
50	**0.326**	0.279	0.208	0.088	0.268	0.084	0.087	0.323
100	**0.346**	0.299	0.218	0.095	0.281	0.091	0.094	0.345
200	0.354	0.31	0.236	0.104	0.3	0.099	0.102	**0.355**
500	0.364	0.334	0.254	0.12	0.33	0.113	0.118	**0.366**
1000	**0.373**	0.36	0.262	0.135	0.35	0.124	0.132	0.37
2000	0.397	0.383	0.28	0.153	0.377	0.137	0.152	**0.4**
5000	**0.439**	0.413	0.289	0.192	0.401	0.16	0.199	0.436

Table 4.1 Mean Average Precision for the SIVAL dataset

N	BoVW k=0	BoVW k=1	BoVW k=2	SPM [126]	mBoVW	mSPM	SPM-D	PM-D
50	**81.2**	77.33	65.73	56.8	78.53	49.33	56.13	80
100	86.67	85.33	75.07	61.2	82.67	54.27	61.6	**89.46**
200	**91.6**	88.4	80.27	63.47	85.47	56.8	65.47	91.07
500	93.07	92	86.67	68.8	90.53	60	69.73	**93.73**
1000	94.67	93.47	88.67	71.2	90.8	61.07	72.4	**96**
2000	95.73	94.67	91.47	73.87	91.2	60.53	74	**96**
5000	96.67	95.07	94.27	74.4	93.33	57.73	75.47	**97.33**

Table 4.2 Classification rates (%) for the SIVAL dataset

N	BoVW k=0	BoVW k=1	BoVW k=2	SPM [126]	mBoVW	mSPM	SPM-D	PM-D
50	0.057	0.041	0.024	0.077	0.038	0.076	**0.08**	0.059
100	0.064	0.047	0.025	0.082	0.043	0.081	**0.086**	0.065
200	0.068	0.05	0.025	0.086	0.045	0.085	**0.09**	0.07
500	0.073	0.052	0.026	0.088	0.048	0.086	**0.094**	0.076
1000	0.077	0.054	0.026	0.088	0.047	0.084	**0.094**	0.081
2000	0.055	0.052	0.027	0.086	0.046	0.081	**0.094**	0.084
5000	0.08	0.052	0.029	0.081	0.045	0.079	**0.089**	0.086

Table 4.3 Mean Average Precision for the Caltech-101 dataset

N	BoVW k=0	BoVW k=1	BoVW k=2	SPM [126]	mBoVW	mSPM	SPM-D	PM-D
50	24.96	21.93	11.04	45.26	20.92	43.09	**45.74**	24.52
100	28.28	25.16	11.41	45.87	23.5	43.9	**47.2**	29.78
200	31.17	27.33	11.85	46.76	24.69	44.58	**47.5**	31.95
500	34.84	28.56	13	45.94	26.49	42.58	**47.23**	35.38
1000	36.26	28.9	12.66	42.78	26.59	38.34	**45.06**	37.35
2000	37.52	28.56	12.56	38.91	26.79	30.46	**41.09**	37.72
5000	37.52	28.59	13.62	27.77	25.29	22.99	31.38	**38.61**

Table 4.4 Classification rates (%) for the Caltech-101 dataset

4.4 Conclusion

In this chapter we were interested in two aspects in visual indexing: the incorporation of spatial context and of multi-resolution/multi-scale strategies in the state-of-the art BoVW approaches. Analysis of the performance of the methods on publicly available databases in both approaches converge to the same conclusions: incorporating information from spatial neighbourhood or from the multi-resolution pyramids into visual content description improves performances. Indeed, in both cases fusion of information coming from different nested layers of local graphs or from different layers of content resolution does bring an improvement in terms of Mean Average Precision (MAP) and classification rates. Obviously the visual scenes/objects to recognize have to be sufficiently rich in terms of quantity of potential characteristic points to ensure a statistical soundness of built visual dictionaries. In the GraphWords approach mixing all BoVWs from singular interest points and local graphs with increasing number of nodes in one description space shows better performances than a "single layer" BoVWs. In the multi-resolution/multi-scale approach building only one dictionary for all levels together is better than building one dictionary per level. In other words, combining the features extracted at different levels of resolution gives the most promising results.

These approaches are far from being totally exhausted. In the GraphWords approach a promising perspective for handling structural deformations of graphs due to occlusions is in the spatial weighting of node features. In a multi-resolution context, intelligent weighting schemes are also needed to tune the importance of local saliencies at different resolution levels. Another perspective is in the use of colour. Indeed the descriptors considered, such as the SURF features, reflect only the "textural" content in the vicinity of characteristic points. The colour has not been considered yet. An interesting way to do it in our vision is to make usage of the local support related to the graphs or to the SURF points themselves. One of the possibilities is in the use of dense features as done in [126]. Furthermore, a direct way of combining both spatial context and multi-resolution would be in a definition of a strategy of combining the layers in graphs with resolution levels in pyramids. Hence the visual content can be indexed with the degree of detail in structure corresponding to its spatial resolution. Furthermore, the use of the high frequency coefficients in the wavelet pyramid can yield computationnaly interesting alternatives to the state-of-the-art SURF and SIFT descriptors in the combined global framework.

Acknowledgements This work was partially supported by ANR 09 BLAN 0165 IMMED grant

Chapter 5
Scalability issues in visual information retrieval

Michel Crucianu

Abstract Information retrieval applications increasingly have to deal with multimedia content. Since image and video databases became ever larger, scalability is a critical requirement for visual information retrieval. This chapter first describes the types of processes that support either content-based retrieval or mining and have to scale. The nature of the problems to be solved and the principle of the solutions are presented next. An emphasis is put on key ideas supporting recent progress, like the use of approximation or of shared-neighbor similarity. To keep the pace with the evolution of scalability requirements, due to more complex visual descriptions and higher volumes of data, further advances are needed. Embeddings, filtering based on simplified descriptions, optimization of content representations and distributed processing are a few directions that deserve being followed.

5.1 Introduction

Visual information retrieval from collections of images or videos is important in many areas, from the social web to video surveillance and from Earth observation to medical imaging. While the contents of such collections can have various domain-specific properties, these collections are increasingly sharing a major characteristic, which is their large size. A few examples allow to better illustrate what is meant here by "large". The digital archive of the Institut National de l'Audiovisuel in France holds more than 4×10^5 hours of audiovisual content. The number of videos on YouTube was estimated to more than 140 millions in 2010. The satellite constellation Pleiades is aimed to provide optical images with a resolution of about 50 cm and to cover up to 10^6 square kilometers per day. For a subset of existing or potential applications it may be possible to select, using e.g. structured metadata, a small share of a collection to subsequently perform visual information retrieval but, given the size of the entire collection, that share can still represent a high volume of content. Furthermore, many new applications such as the analysis of climate-related trends in an Earth observation image archive are only meaningful if a broad set of data is employed.

Consequently, core processes like content-based retrieval and mining must be able to work with very large volumes of visual content. In this context, a process is considered to be "scalable" if it can be easily extended to handle a much larger set of data and its overall consumption of resources increases gracefully with the size of the database. Applications involving visual information retrieval can hardly be economically viable if the processes they require are not all scalable. To make these processes scalable we have to consider various problems, briefly outlined in Section 5.2.

Scalability of visual information retrieval has been a concern for the last two decades and principled approaches for solving these problems were put forward, see Section 5.3. While most of the work focused on scalable retrieval (5.3.1), problems more directly concerning mining are being increasingly addressed (5.3.2).

The scalability requirements progressively but significantly evolved with the size of the collections and also with the nature of the data. Indeed, to improve the quality of retrieval results, more comprehensive and refined descriptions of the visual content were proposed. This also made the comparison of descriptions more complex, asking for key extensions to existing methods that support scalability (5.4.1). To further improve scalability, an important direction is the joint optimization of content description and indexing (5.4.2), possibly for each specific database. Last but not least, using distributed data and resources both brings new opportunities and raises new challenges for scalable visual information retrieval (5.4.3).

5.2 Scalable Retrieval and Mining: A Typology of Problems

Most of the expensive processes in visual information retrieval concern the computation of distances, similarities, kernels, etc. between visual descriptions, together with the transfer of these descriptions from mass storage if they do not all hold into the main memory. Let us consider some frequent operations and their corresponding *basic* time complexity, i.e. when scalability requirements are ignored. Consider $\mathcal{D}$ is the database of visual descriptions employed and N is the cardinality of $\mathcal{D}$.

The "query by example" method allows to retrieve the objects whose descriptions are similar to the description of a query object. Most frequently employed are the ε-range queries, where an upper bound ε is provided for the distance and the expected result is $\mathcal{S}_\varepsilon(q) = \{x \in c | d(x,q) \le \varepsilon\}$, together with the k nearest neighbors (kNN) queries, where an upper bound k is provided for the number of nearest neighbors to be returned and the result should be $\mathcal{K}_k(q) = \{x \in \mathcal{D} | |\mathcal{K}_k(q)| = k \wedge \forall y \in \mathcal{D} - \mathcal{K}_k(q), d(y,q) \ge d(x,q)\}$. The basic time complexity of these retrieval operations is $O(N)$, corresponding to the case where all the descriptions in the database are compared to the description of the query (exhaustive or "sequential" search).

To take a decision regarding an object on the basis of its k nearest neighbors requires the identification of these neighbors. To estimate a probability density function in some point with Parzen windows we need to compute kernels between that point and the descriptions in the database. The basic time complexity of these operations is also $O(N)$ (if computing a kernel is $O(1)$). To evaluate the decision function for an object with a kernel machine requires the computation of kernels between the description of the object and other specific descriptions (e.g. the support vectors), which has a basic time complexity of $O(n)$ where n is the number of these other descriptions.

In some semi-supervised learning methods like SVM-based transduction, it may be necessary to find the unlabeled data that is closest to the discrimination boundary. In active learning, one well known criterion for the selection of data for labeling is ambiguousness, also requiring to return the unlabeled data that is closest to the current discrimination boundary. In both cases the basic time complexity is $O(N)$. Note however that the query is a boundary, so it has a different nature than the objects in the database.

To find in a database all the variants of a same content (with slight changes) requires a similarity self-join $\mathcal{J}_\theta = \{(x,y) \mid x, y \in \mathcal{D}, d(x,y) \le \theta\}$. In a metric space, finding clusters in the data relies on the computation of pairwise distances between data points. Both operations typically have a basic time complexity of $O(N^2)$. Also, to perform supervised learning with a kernel machine we need to compute kernels between all the pairs of labeled data objects, which has a complexity of $O(n^2)$ where n is the size of the training dataset.

To summarize, we can distinguish two broad process families: (i) retrieval of the objects that are similar to a query having the same or a different nature than the objects in the database, and (ii) all-pairs comparisons. Even though basic time complexity is only linear in N for processes from the first family, this is still too expensive for large databases. Fortunately, for such processes it is usually possible to make the overall consumption of resources increase sublinearly with the size of the database. Similar methods also allow to reduce the time complexity of processes from the second family. The ideas underlying such complexity reductions are outlined next.

5.3 Principled Approaches to Scalability

The retrieval of the data that is most similar to a query (ε-range or kNN) should not be concerned with data objects that are "too far" from the query. Also, since kernels are significantly different from zero only for neighboring data, computing kernels for data objects that are "too far" from each other is likely to be useless. If the major part of the database is "too far" to be relevant for the current query or kernel evaluation, then we can significantly reduce computation costs by filtering out as early as possible large distant segments of data. This is the key idea supporting scalability in this domain. To put this idea into practice, many data structures and corresponding access methods were designed, aiming to reduce the order of complexity of the retrieval or mining process.

Starting from the well known B+ tree or from hashing, originally employed for unidimensional attributes un relational databases, various methods were put forward for spatial databases and then for multimedia databases; the research monograph [185] provides a comprehensive view. While the key idea is simple, the nature of visual descriptions and of the associated distances, similarity measures or kernels raises serious difficulties in finding how to filter out efficiently large distant segments of data. First, descriptions of visual content are often high-dimensional vectors. The *curse of dimensionality* is the generic name given to a set of phenomena that occur for high-dimensional data and hinder access methods; they will be further described in subsection 5.3.1. In the extreme case where data follows a uniform or unimodal distribution in an area of a high-dimensional space, kNN retrieval becomes meaningless because the kNN of a query are not significantly closer to the query than the rest of the data (see [21]).

Second, many descriptions of visual content are not individual vectors but more complex objects like sets of vectors (sometimes with associated configuration information) or plane graphs. While it is usually possible to define distances or kernels between such descriptions, simple vector representations are not appropriate for them, so access methods defined for vector spaces cannot be applied. Moreover, the computation of these distances or kernels is complex. Recent proposals addressing these problems are outlined in subsection 5.4.1.

An important component of the cost of a retrieval or mining process corresponds to the transfer of visual descriptions from mass storage if they do not all hold into the main memory. Given the fact that random access to data in main memory is on average 10^5 times faster than random access on disks and $2 \cdot 10^4$ times faster than random access on SDD, the cost of access to mass storage is usually dominating distance or kernel computations. We may be able to avoid accesses to mass storage by distributing a large database together with distance or kernel computations on a set of computers such that all the data holds in the distributed main memory (see 5.4.3). It is also important to note that *sequential* access to data on disk or SSD has a similar cost to random access to main memory, as this has a non-negligible impact on the design and evaluation of access methods.

5.3.1 Scalable Retrieval

For the retrieval of the objects that are similar to a query, the goal is to reduce complexity from $O(N)$ to $O(\log N)$ or even $O(1)$ by filtering out as early as possible large distant segments of data. We will focus here on the main approaches that were successfully employed for visual content in the recent years. They can be applied to "query by example" retrieval, but also to kNN-based decision making, to probability density function estimation with Parzen windows or to the evaluation of decision functions for kernel machines.

The first popular approach for dealing with ε-range queries consists in (i) building off-line a search tree based on a hierarchical partitioning of the data or of the description space, then (ii) performing retrieval online by recursively following the tree structure and pruning branches that do not intersect the query. Since the height of the tree is $O(\log N)$, if all branches but one are pruned starting from the root then complexity can be reduced from $O(N)$ to $O(\log N)$. When mass storage is needed and considering that each node of the tree holds on a memory page (unit of transfer from mass storage to main memory), then the number of disk reads shows a similar reduction in complexity compared to exhaustive search. In practice, depending on characteristics of the database and of the specific data structure employed, several branches may have to be explored in the traversed nodes, so actual complexity is higher than the lower bound $O(\log N)$. To retrieve the kNN of a query it is possible to rely on the ε-range algorithm in the following way: a set of k neighbors is initialized to a random selection of data objects, then the distance of the farthest of these objects to the query is taken as ε and an ε-range retrieval is started; every time an object is found that has a distance to the query μ smaller than the current value of ε, it replaces the farthest neighbor in the current list of k neighbors and the new value of ε is reduced to μ before pursuing ε-range retrieval.

Many data structures follow this first approach. Most of them require vectorial data, but some only need a metric space (e.g. the M-tree [48] and its evolutions). They either perform space partitioning (e.g. the k-d-B-tree [178]) or data partitioning (e.g. the SR-tree [118], M-tree [48] or cover tree [22]). Space partitioning allows to avoid overlap between partitions at the same level of the hierarchy and can be interesting when the data fills well a regular area in the description space. Data partitioning is preferable when the distribution of data is very irregular but, since the partitions need to have a simple shape in order to support pruning, partitions at the same level of the hierarchy can overlap. Data objects that fall in such overlapping areas between partitions are typically stored in only one partition to save space, but if the query range intersects such an area then all the partitions containing this area have to be explored.

Most of the methods following the first approach are designed to perform *exact* retrieval. However, it is also possible to provide approximate results to a query. For example, if $\mathcal{K}_k(q)$ is the set of true k nearest neighbors of a query q and $r_k = \max_{x \in \mathcal{K}_k(q)} d(x,q)$, then an approximation to the set of kNN of q can be defined as $\mathcal{K}_{k,\beta}(q) = \{x \in \mathcal{D} \mid |\mathcal{K}_{k,\beta}(q)| = k \wedge \forall x \in \mathcal{K}_{k,\beta}(q), d(x,q) \leq (1+\beta)r_k\}$, where $\beta > 0$ controls the approximation. In many application contexts, especially when there is a semantic gap between image description and user intention, visual information retrieval can accept approximate retrieval results. Many methods designed to perform exact retrieval can be modified to provide instead approximate results and this usually allows to reduce retrieval costs. As an example, for approximate kNN retrieval defined as above, more branches of a tree can be pruned during search since an improvement of the set of NN that reduces the range below the current ε but not below $\frac{\varepsilon}{1+\beta}$ is useless.

Hashing is extensively employed in relational databases because it allows to reduce complexity from $O(N)$ to $O(1)$ for exact matches, but classical hash functions were inappropriate for retrieval by similarity since similar (but not identical) data objects usually had different hash keys. *Locality-sensitive* hashing (LSH) was introduced in [80] as a scalable similarity-based *approximate* retrieval method, with a time complexity shown to be sublinear in the size of the database and linear in the dimension of data. After various extensions, hashing became the most successfully employed approach to visual content retrieval. Let $\mathcal{X}$ be the domain to which the data in the database $\mathcal{D}$ belongs, $\mathcal{Q}$ a set of keys and $d_{\mathcal{H}} : \mathcal{X} \times \mathcal{X} \to \mathbb{R}^+$ a metric on $\mathcal{X}$. Then $\mathcal{H} = h : \mathcal{X} \to \mathcal{Q}$ is a family of (r_1, r_2, p_1, p_2)-sensitive hash functions [80] if $\forall x, y \in \mathcal{X}$, if $d(x, y) \le r_1$ then $P_{h \in \mathcal{H}}(h(x) = h(y)) \ge p_1$ and if $d(x, y) > r_2$ then $P_{h \in \mathcal{H}}(h(x) = h(y)) \le p_2$ (useful when $r_2 > r_1 > 0$ and $p_1 > p_2 > 0$). With a locality-sensitive hash function, similar objects are likely to have a same hash key while dissimilar objects are likely to have different hash keys. LSH families were put forward for many metrics, including L_p or Hamming, and various similarity measures, like cosine similarity or set similarity.

An LSH family $\mathcal{H}$ can be employed for retrieval by similarity in the following way: (i) several ordered subsets of functions in $\mathcal{H}$ are selected; every subset has the same number of functions and defines a hash table; (ii) every object in $\mathcal{D}$ is hashed with the functions in each subset and the object reference is stored, in each table, in the case (or *bucket*) corresponding to the resulting key for that table; a key is the concatenation of the hash keys provided by the functions in the ordered subset of that table; (iii) when a query object q is given, it is also hashed with the functions in each subset and all the objects in the buckets associated to the resulting keys are returned. This filtering stage can be followed by the computation of the distance to the query for each of the returned objects. Since with a single hash table two similar data objects don't necessarily have a same key, to obtain a high recall we have to employ a very large number of independent hash tables, which has a negative impact on the scalability of retrieval. An important reduction in the number of hash tables required can be obtained by defining neighborhoods for the keys (based on the neighborhoods of their data domains) and also probing, for each query, the keys that are neighbors with the key of the query (multi-probe LSH [135]. The number of neighbors to be probed can be significantly reduced by exploiting estimated *a posteriori* probabilities of finding relevant data in these neighbors (*a posteriori* multi-probe LSH [111]). Further improvements rely on making the selection of hash functions *data-dependent*, see subsection 5.4.2.

A major issue in using data structures and associated access methods to improve the scalability of retrieval by similarity is the curse of dimensionality. Among the various phenomena that characterize high-dimensional data, we only mention a few that have a negative impact on data structures and associated access methods. First, for space partitioning methods, when the dimension d of the data increases, the number of partitions increases exponentially, which strongly reduces the efficiency of retrieval. Second, data in some region of space gets closer to the external boundary of that region: the probability of being at less than δ from the boundary is $1 - (1 - 2\delta)^d$. Third, as shown in [21], if the data follows a uniform or unimodal distribution in an area of space, when data dimension increases the difference between the smallest distance between data objects and the largest distance decreases. For data partitioning methods, these two phenomena lead to an increase in the overlap between same level partitions and, also, to an increase of the number of partitions that intersect the range of a query. The consequence is again a reduction of the retrieval efficiency. If neighboring data objects are not much closer than the rest of the data objects, it is more difficult to filter out large distant segments of data. At some point, the access method becomes less efficient than exhaustive search. Depending on the method, this can happen for d between about 8 and 20. If the dimension increases much more, the variance of the distance distribution vanishes and looking for the kNN of a query becomes meaningless [21]. Real data typically has a multi-modal distribution, so the reduction in retrieval efficiency occurs for higher dimensions, but is nevertheless present. It is important to note that the dimension that matters is not the one of the vector space in which the data objects are represented but rather the intrinsic dimension of the available data. Indeed, if the data represented in a high-dimensional space actually spans a low-dimensional manifold, data distribution will correspond to the dimension of the manifold rather than to the dimension of the entire space.

The fact that data is not defined in a vector space (so we cannot speak of data dimension) but belongs to a metric space does not remove difficulties: if the variance of the distance distribution is small compared to the average, then a metric data partitioning method like the M-tree also becomes inefficient.

Approximation can improve scalability in the difficult cases when the distance distribution has a small variance but kNN retrieval is still meaningful. This was experimentally shown for various data structures and associated access methods, like approximate kNN retrieval with the M-tree [47]. To explain this finding we note that the pruning condition is stricter, so more branches are pruned earlier, and that the retrieval algorithm can safely stop when a lower bound is reached for the similarity to a query. The lower bound is large for high-dimensional data since the variance of the distance distribution decreases while the average distance increases with data dimension d. The importance of approximation was also demonstrated with the introduction of LSH, for which the time complexity is provably sublinear in N and linear in d. Interesting scalability results were also obtained by using shared-neighbor similarity measures instead of global similarity for high-dimensional data [100].

5.3.2 Scalable Mining

Data mining is increasingly employed in support of visual information retrieval. Supervised, active and semi-supervised learning allow to build concept detectors, sometimes interactively defined by user feedback. Similarity joins and cluster analysis make possible the development of intermediate-level descriptions that are closer than low level features to the semantics of user queries. The scalability of the expensive processes involved in mining is being more directly addressed.

In active learning, data ambiguousness is a popular criterion for the selection of data for labeling; ambiguous unlabeled data is close to the current discrimination boundary. In SVM-based transduction (semi-supervised learning), in order to take unlabeled data into account when maximizing the margin, it is necessary to find which unlabeled data objects are close to the current discrimination boundary and can thus have an impact on the margin. The problem to solve is to efficiently find the k data objects nearest to the boundary or all the data objects within a range around the boundary.

The use of a boundary as query is both conceptually and computationally more difficult than the use of an object as query (point query). Since the boundary has a complex shape in the description space it is not possible to directly compute a distance between a data object and the boundary. It was nevertheless suggested in [161] to use a data structure in the description space and return data in the neighborhood of either positive or negative examples; this is only a first stage of filtering, followed by the computation of the decision function for all the resulting data. The boundary is thus progressively approached by neighborhoods of existing examples.

Some methods take advantage of the fact that for kernel machines like SVM the boundary is a hyperplane in the feature space generated by the kernel. In [162] the selection stage for active learning with SVM relies on the use of clustering in feature space and on the selection of the clusters that are nearest to the hyperplane corresponding to the discrimination boundary. A new data structure, KDX, is also introduced: since for most of the kernels employed one has $K(x,x) = \alpha$ for some fixed α, the feature space representations of all the data objects are on a hypersphere of radius α. These representations are then distributed in rings around a central vector, and these rings are indexed according to the angle to the central vector. A second-level data structure is used within each ring. For any query, KDX performs intra and inter-ring pruning. Another method aimed to support scalability for boundary queries was suggested in [52]: an M-tree is built in the feature space and M-tree access methods (including approximate kNN retrieval) are extended to "hyperplane queries" that aim to find the k nearest neighbors of a hyperplane. The fact that the feature space is high-dimensional (potentially infinite dimensional, depending on the kernel) is not necessarily a problem, since the images in feature space of the data objects may span a low dimensional manifold. But a hyperplane is much less selective than a point query and this significantly reduces the efficiency of the access method.

Active learning is often employed for retrieval with *relevance feedback* (RF). This is an interactive and iterative retrieval method that consists in asking the user to provide feedback, at each iteration, regarding the relevance of the results returned by the system, and in using this feedback to improve the estimation of the retrieval target by the system. First introduced for text documents, RF rapidly developed for image retrieval, mainly because a user can quickly evaluate the relevance of an image. For a retrieval session with RF, the target class of data usually represents a very small share of the database (which is not the case for active learning in general), so the decision boundary is not far from the positive examples. It follows that the most ambiguous data objects are likely to be found among the kNN of already labeled positive examples. This idea is successfully developed in [81] with LSH-based approximate kNN retrieval.

Supervised learning with a kernel machine requires the computation of kernels between all the pairs of training data objects. However, most kernels are significantly different from zero only for neighboring data, so it is useless to compute kernels for data objects that are too distant from each other. To cluster data that is not defined in a vector space but belongs to a metric space, existing methods rely on the computation of pairwise distances between data points. Computing the distance between data points that are too far from each other to belong to a same cluster is a waste of time. To find what data objects in one database $\mathcal{D}_1$ are similar to data objects in another database $\mathcal{D}_2$ requires a similarity join $\mathcal{J}_\theta(\mathcal{D}_1, \mathcal{D}_2) = \{(x, y) | x \in \mathcal{D}_1, y \in \mathcal{D}_2, d(x, y) \leq \theta\}$. Similarity joins can also be defined using the kNN rather than a distance threshold. If $\mathcal{D}_1 = \mathcal{D}_2$ then we have a similarity self-join. With an appropriate similarity threshold, similarity self-joins can also be employed as a first selection stage for kernel computations in supervised learning and for data clustering.

The basic time complexity of a similarity self-join is $O(N^2)$ (when a comparison is performed for every pair of data objects) and the goal is to reduce this complexity to $O(N \log N)$ or less. It is important to note that the overall complexity of similarity self-joins is necessarily higher than the size of the result $\mathcal{J}_\theta(\mathcal{D}_1, \mathcal{D}_2)$. So, if most of the data points are closer to each other than the threshold θ, or if all distances between data points are comparable and do not allow to define a meaningful value for θ, then no reduction in complexity can be expected. This last situation occurs when the variance of the distance distribution vanishes, e.g. for data having a very high intrinsic dimension.

A first general approach for performing scalable similarity joins consists in the direct application of scalable retrieval solutions: every object in the database is used as a θ-range query and a scalable retrieval method is employed to find the data in that range. If the complexity of retrieval is $O(\log N)$, then this generic method allows to perform similarity joins in $O(N \log N)$ time. Neighbors of different data objects are being searched for *independently*; it is possible to do better by taking similarity correlations into account.

The method suggested in [176] consists in (i) building a search tree based on a hierarchical partitioning of the data, then (ii) performing a hierarchical comparison of the tree nodes. If two nodes are found to be too far from each other, then no comparison is needed between their descendants. The best-case time complexity of stage (ii) is $O(N)$. Even though stage (i) has a complexity of $O(N \log N)$, it only needs to be carried out once, then stage (ii) can be performed every time a join with a different threshold is required.

Several methods rely on the fact that a data object can be described as a set of tokens and these tokens can be globally ordered according to a natural criterion. If the similarity between two documents is above a threshold, then their prefixes (ordered strings of tokens) should share tokens, so inverted lists of tokens can be employed for the join. Several methods for exact similarity joins rely on prefix filtering and add complementary criteria. The PPJoin+ method in [226] adds a positional filtering criterion based on a relation between the position of common tokens and an upper bound on the similarity. This method was successfully employed for near duplicate detection in large databases of text documents.

A different approach, performing *approximate* similarity self-joins, was put forward in [171] and applied to finding the variants of video segments in a database. It is based on dividing the entire database into segments such that, in each segment, the similarity between any two data objects is above a threshold, and then performing the similarity self-join independently for every segment. In a large database the data objects are scattered rather than grouped into compact and well separated clusters, so different segments must overlap in order to guarantee a recall of 1 (i.e. all the similar pairs are found). Redundancy is controlled in order to obtain a good trade-off between effectiveness (high recall) and efficiency (low computation cost).

5.3.3 How to Evaluate Scalability

The methods performing exact retrieval by similarity (or exact similarity joins), if correctly implemented, return the same results as exhaustive search (respectively as joins based on exhaustive comparisons). Only their efficiency has to be evaluated. For the methods returning approximate results, the quality of these results with respect to those obtained by exact methods (the *effectiveness*) should also be measured.

Efficiency is characterized by comparison with at least exhaustive search (or exhaustive joins) and, if possible, with other reference methods. While lower and upper bounds on the complexity are in many cases available, these bounds do not allow to obtain reliable estimates of the efficiency on real databases with specific data distributions. Experimental comparisons are then needed. It is important to perform the evaluations for several databases of increasing size in order to obtain an experimental estimate of the complexity and not only measure the cost at fixed size.

In measuring the efficiency of retrieval, a distinction must be made between the response time for individual queries and the cost per query when a large batch of queries is processed. For applications requiring interactivity the response time is the major concern, while the other applications are rather interested by a minimum cost per query. Batch processing can be optimized by organizing the queries so as to minimize the impact of data exchanges between main memory and mass storage.

For approximate methods, theoretical bounds on effectiveness are more difficult to obtained. The returned results should be experimentally compared to those of an exact method. This can be done for the results returned by ε-range queries, kNN queries or similarity joins, using precision and recall, the ground truth being defined by the exact method. For example, the true kNN of a specific query are found by an exact method (at worst, by exhaustive search), then the set of approximate kNN returned by the method to evaluate is compared to this set of true kNN. When the number of objects returned is the same as the number of objects in the "class", i.e. k, precision and recall both correspond to the ratio between the number of true kNN found by the approximate method and k. Another measure of effectiveness is the ratio between the sum of distances to the approximate kNN and the sum of distances to the true kNN. Recall is stricter than this measure: even if the approximate kNN are almost as close to the query as the true kNN, if there is little overlap between the two sets then recall is low. Since the cost of finding the true kNN for very many queries (or for all the data objects in the database, considered as queries) can be very high, especially if exhaustive search has to be employed, a representative sample of queries can be used and provides a partial ground truth. For the evaluation of similarity joins, the partial ground truth used to estimate performances can be obtained by selecting a sample of subsets of data objects and limiting the exhaustive join to the data in these subsets.

To be representative for the later use of the methods under evaluation, experiments should be performed on real databases having the same general characteristics and same order of magnitude as those on which the methods are expected to be employed. Indeed, significant differences exist between the distributions of data descriptions of different types or obtained on very different databases; these differences can have a strong impact on the efficiency and effectiveness of access methods. Also, the storage hierarchy can behave differently for data structures of very different sizes. Setting up large databases of images or video is facing important difficulties, like rights protection issues, which explains why past evaluation campaigns did not explicitly address scalability. We can nevertheless mention an increase in the volumes of video employed in the high level concept detection task of TREC Video Retrieval Evaluation (TRECVID, see Section 6.3.1), as well as recent successful initiatives that explicitly address scalability, like http://corpus-texmex.irisa.fr.

5.4 Trends in Scalable Visual Information Retrieval

The ever larger image and video databases, together with the steady development of refined visual descriptions, lead to increasingly stronger scalability requirements for visual information retrieval. In the following we attempt to identify a few trends regarding the ability to exploit complex descriptions, the optimization of content description and indexing, and the use of distributed data and resources.

5.4.1 Complex Data

Early descriptions of visual content were high-dimensional vectors representing global image characteristics (e.g. distribution of colors or of edge orientations) and compared using simple metrics like L_1 or L_2. To solve complex problems in pattern recognition and visual information retrieval, more comprehensive and refined descriptions were progressively developed, based on local or semi-local features with various invariance properties. Images are typically described by large sets of such features, with additional information regarding the positions and orientations of the features in the image. Comparisons frequently involve complex metrics between (sub)sets of features, matching via an affine transform, kernels taking geometry into account or graph kernels (see Section 4.2). This raises two problems. First, classic data structures and associated access methods may not be adequate for such data or such comparisons. Second, every single comparison can have a high computation cost. While metric data structures like the M-tree can in principle be employed when the comparison relies on a metric, they prove to be inefficient for metrics that are so expensive to compute.

A generic solution to both problems is to define embeddings. Consider the visual descriptions are defined in a metric space $(\mathcal{M}, d_{\mathcal{M}})$, then we must find a normed space $\mathcal{N}$ (typically $\mathbb{R}^d$ for some appropriate d) and a mapping $f : \mathcal{M} \to \mathcal{N}$ such that the original distance between any two data objects $x, y \in \mathcal{M}$ is comparable to the distance $d_{\mathcal{N}}$ defined on $\mathcal{N}$ as the norm of the difference between their images $f(x), f(y) \colon d_{\mathcal{N}} = \|f(x) - f(y)\|_{\mathcal{N}}$. A data structure with an efficient access method can then be employed in $\mathcal{N}$ (so the first problem is solved) and complex computations of $d_{\mathcal{M}}$ are replaced by simpler computations of $d_{\mathcal{N}}$ (so the second problem is solved). There are however some issues: (i) a low distorsion embedding has to be found, (ii) retrieval can only be approximate since the distortions are not zero, (iii) the mapping f should be easy to compute. Low distorsion embeddings do not exist for important comparison measures that are not metrics. Examples provided in [23] for the Bhattacharyya and the Kullback-Leibler divergences show that tentative embeddings into a metric space can incur arbitrarily large distortions. A different, kernel-based hashing solution for symmetric *non-metric* dissimilarity measures (like the symmetrized Bregman divergence) was recently suggested in [154].

Various solutions using embeddings were proposed for effective and efficient similarity-based visual content retrieval, see for example [104] where the Earth-Mover Distance (EMD) is embedded into $\mathbb{R}^d$ with the L_1 metric and LSH is then applied in $\mathbb{R}^d$.

But embeddings are not the only possible solution. Actually, the requirements of low distorsion embeddings are too strong. A data structure and associated access method are only needed for performing an *efficient filtering* of the database. This filtering must simply return a small enough pool of good candidates so as to reduce the overall cost of the subsequent computation of the complex metrics, of the matching or of the kernel for all the candidates in this pool; also, filtering out good candidates should be avoided. Methods taking advantage of this fact are both efficient and easy to set up, so one can expect them to develop further.

In cases where matching via an affine transform may eventually have to be computed, methods like min-wise independent permutations locality sensitive hashing (MinHash) proved to be good filtering solutions [46]. For a set of local features that are close to each other in the image plane, MinHash efficiently finds all the images containing similar sets of features. This information can be discriminant enough, even in a large database, to allow the selection of a small enough pool of candidate images. A rather similar method, based on local triples of local features but adding a simple information regarding the geometry of the triple, was shown to provide high selectivity for similarity self-joins on a large database of video keyframes [172].

To improve the scalability of processes that require kernel computations, a generic method was put forward in [121]. It consists in applying LSH in the feature space associated to the kernel. The standard LSH solution requires to draw from a Gaussian distribution the normal vector to the hyperplane defining a hash function. This cannot be done directly in the feature space if the mapping between description space and feature space is unknown or incomputable, which is the case for many widely used kernels. The solution consists in using the Central Limit Theorem: the mean of sufficiently many independent identically distributed samples converges to a Gaussian distribution. Hyperplanes in feature space are then defined by normal vectors that are means of a relatively large number of other vectors. While this requires a more expensive computation for each hash function, the method is generic with respect to the kernels. It was nevertheless shown [112] that, since convergence is slow, resulting hash functions are not independent enough, which degrades performance.

In the method proposed in [112], also applicable to any kernel, each hash function is obtained by maximizing the margin in feature space between two random samples of the data. This strongly improves independence between hash functions, even when the number of hash functions required is very large, which this leads to better effectiveness and efficiency. Note that, while these proposals can be applied to any kernel, they still require kernel computations.

5.4.2 Optimized Representations and Scalability

We have seen that, in order to support scalable retrieval or mining, a data structure and associated access method only have to efficiently filter the data. More complex distance or kernel computations are subsequently performed on the selected candidates. This also implies that filtering can be performed on data representations that are just *sufficient* to support reliable filtering. Such representations can then be significantly more compact than the original descriptions of the visual content. To be useful, these compact representations (or codes) must reflect the similarity between original descriptions at the scale where filtering takes place. This is a form of embedding, but where a large part of the low distortion constraints are relaxed (see e.g. [107]).

Hashing is an important and broad family of methods that allow to obtain such codes. The set of hash functions corresponding to hash table provides a key for an original description. The code of that description is obtained by concatenating the hash keys provided by the sets of hash functions associated to the different hash tables being employed. Since the hash functions are locality-sensitive, the resulting code does represent a form of embedding.

There are several important distinctions among hashing methods (see also [112]). In the early proposals (e.g. [80]) and some of the more recent ones, the definition of the hash function family only depends on the description space and on the similarity measure considered; while data distributions have no impact on this definition, they can be used during the retrieval stage like in *a posteriori* multi-probe LSH [111] to improve efficiency for similar effectiveness.

The number of hash functions required for obtaining some level of effectiveness can be reduced if the hash family depends on the data distribution. Unsupervised data dependent hashing methods only consider the distribution of data and no supervision information. Spectral hashing [223] directly attempts to obtain binary codes for data descriptions by optimizing the correspondence between the affinities of data objects and the affinities of associated binary codes. While effectiveness is improved over LSH for small codes, the different bits are not independent enough and this degrades performance for longer codes. The proposal in [112] is focused on improving the independence between the selected hash functions, defined in the feature space associated to a kernel: each function is obtained by maximizing the margin between two random samples of the data. When the data distribution is stationary, data dependent hashing methods like the one in [112] can provide more compact codes than data independent hashing, with both better effectiveness and improved efficiency. For non-stationary data distributions, data independent hashing can be expected to be more robust.

Some hashing methods further take into account task-related supervision information like class labels or pairwise constraints in order to optimize the selected set of hash functions. In [184], stacked Restricted Boltzmann Machines learn an auto-encoding task and obtain compact binary codes (in a hidden layer) for input data descriptions. These codes preserve the neighborhood structure of the input data and can be used as hash keys. In a second stage of learning, labeled data can be employed and network weights are modified to minimize classification errors, which also leads to refined binary codes taking into account the "semantic" similarity provided by the labels.

The semi-supervised hashing method proposed in [222] is a data-dependent projection learning problem, where both class labels of training data objects and known similarities between data objects are translated into must-link or cannot-link pairwise constraints. Hash functions producing binary keys are then obtained by minimizing the error on the set of constraints while enforcing balanced partitioning of the database and orthogonality between hash functions. The proposal in [153] also translates both class labels of training data and known similarities between data objects into pairwise constraints. Hashing is defined in the feature space associated to a kernel. The cost function employs margin-based regularization and includes a penalty to enforce the consistency between hashing partitions and pairwise constraints.

The method put forward in [130] minimizes Kullback-Leibler divergence between the affinity matrix of the original data and the affinity matrix of the binary hash codes. When labeled data is available, the affinity matrix of the original data is obtained by computing similarities between data objects belonging to a same class; data objects in different classes are assigned zero similarity. A new hash function (a new bit for the codes) is generated by minimizing its mutual information with the existing hash functions.

Problem-related supervision information like class labels or pairwise constraints supports a reduction in code length with respect to unsupervised hashing, but this is achieved by removing other information from these codes. For example, the codes may no longer be able to discriminate classes that are not present in the initial labeled data. Aware of this potential drawback, several of the suggested methods attempt to balance "semantic" similarities provided by class labels or pairwise constraints available for part of the data and metric information that is present for all the data.

5.4.3 Distributed Data and Resources

The distribution of computation and storage over a large number of computers has the potential to significantly improve scalability in visual information retrieval but also raises new challenges. First, response time is strongly diminished if parallel computations are possible, even though the order of complexity cannot be reduced. Second, online accesses to mass storage may become unnecessary if all the required data holds in the main memory cumulated over all the computers involved; this has a positive impact both on response time and on the total cost. The main challenges concern the construction and maintenance of a distributed data structure, load balancing to optimize parallelism, or the replication of data and computation to face local failures, while keeping system overhead low.

Many distributed data structures and associated access methods were proposed, but very few were evaluated with large databases of visual descriptions. Moreover, different distributed infrastructures can raise specific problems so the results obtained in one context may be hard to extend to another context. For example, computers in a cluster are typically homogeneous, are connected by high bandwidth networks and can follow a central controller. In a peer-to-peer system, computers are usually heterogeneous, are connected by low speed and potentially unreliable networks, can connect or disconnect from the network at any moment, and control is often distributed. We consider here two recent proposals that were rather extensively evaluated, one on a structured peer-to-peer infrastructure and the other on a cloud computing infrastructure.

Similarity search on a test collection of up to 100 million images, using centralized and distributed metric data structures with associated access methods, is described in [14]. The image collection (CoPhIR) considered comprises 50×10^6 Flickr images described by MPEG-7 global features. For progressively larger sizes of the database, different systems are defined and evaluated. A general requirement is to always have a response time of less than 1.5 seconds in order to support truly interactive search. For a database of 10^5 images, a centralized system is sufficient. The data structure employed is Pivoting M-tree with an improved node-splitting algorithm proposed for the Slim-Tree. All the data holds in main memory. For a database size of 10^6, a distributed system is required. M-Chord is the distributed data structure allowing to identify, for each query, which peers are concerned. Every peer is using a local M-tree data structure to store the descriptions it was allocated and to answer the queries it receives; all its data holds into main memory. For a database of 10^7 images the M-Chord is again employed as distributed data structure, but with an approximate retrieval method that only examines highly-promising data partitions and ignores partitions having low probability of containing relevant data. For a database size of 50×10^6 (or higher) the same data structures and access methods are employed, but the leaf nodes of the local M-tree of every peer are stored on disk. In spite of this, the response time remains within 1.4 seconds and recall is above 80%. Since a single query does not fully use the CPUs, the system is estimated able to process about 30 queries in parallel. Evaluations shows that the same data structures can be used at several scales of the data and of the distributed system, requiring nevertheless adaptations mainly consisting in the introduction of approximations. The overall system is demonstrated online with 100×10^6 images on the web page of the Multi-Feature Indexing Network (MUFIN) project, http://mufin.fi.muni.cz.

Since cloud computing is receiving increasing attention as a general framework for scalable processing, it is important to see to what extent such an infrastructure is adequate for visual information retrieval. In [13] a new metric data structure was put forward together with associated approximate retrieval methods. The data structure, designed to allow parallel operations, is based on pivots and inverted lists. The construction of the index (the data structure) and similarity-based retrieval were then implemented in a Hadoop framework using HDFS and HBase. The evaluation was performed on a database of 2×10^9 local features (SIFT) using a 15 computer cluster. The results show that a good level of parallelism can be obtained, potentially supporting a high throughput. However, the default job starting overhead due to the framework is relatively high and has a negative impact on the response time that is of several seconds. To better support interactive retrieval, the framework and the retrieval method must be specifically tuned to reduce this overhead.

5.5 Conclusion

While scalability of visual information retrieval has been a concern for about two decades and principled approaches were put forward quite early, solutions for databases of realistic size were only proposed in the recent years. Key to the latest progress was the acknowledgement of the fact that approximation was perfectly acceptable for retrieval by similarity and could lead to significant reductions in computation cost. Most of the work on scalability focused on retrieval, but problems concerning mining are being increasingly addressed.

The more extensive use of refined visual descriptions with complex comparison operations raised new scalability difficulties. Low distorsion embeddings were a first solution to this problem. A second solution consists in using data structures and associated access methods for an efficient and effective filtering on simplified data representations, and only performing complex comparisons for the remaining candidates.

Increasingly stronger scalability requirements come from the need to make the most of ever larger image and video databases. For multi-level processing, the optimization of visual content representations with respect to data distributions and to the problem to be solved should continue to support significant advances. Distributed processing is another important direction to follow for scalable visual information retrieval.

While the recent progress in this domain is encouraging, it is important to keep in mind the rate at which the amount of available multimedia content increases.

Chapter 6
Evaluation of visual information indexing and retrieval

Georges Quénot, Philippe Joly

Abstract Comparative evaluation of methods and systems is of primarily importance in the domain of visual indexing and retrieval. As in many other domains, it is generally organized by institutions like NIST or by research networks like Pascal or PetaMedia. Evaluations are carried out in the context of periodical campaigns, or benchmarks. In these, one or more visual indexing or retrieval tasks are defined, each with a data collection, relevance judgments, performance measures and an experimentation protocol. Participants submit results computed automatically and blindly and the organizers return the measured performances. These evaluation campaigns are generally concluded by a workshop in which the participants explain how they performed the tasks. The chapter will give an overview of the major evaluation campaigns in the domain and present in detail the tasks, the data collection, the metrics and the protocols used. The state of the art performance in recent campaigns and the lessons learned from these campaigns will also be presented.

6.1 Introduction

Indexing visual contents requires a large set of atomic technologies, each of them being the scope of research works. To develop and to assess these works, a minimal content set is generally collected and annotated to test the relevance of the propositions. But most of the time, this content set cannot be distributed and therefore results cannot be verified — at least in strictly the same conditions than the ones used in the experimental framework — while reviewing the proposed works. On the base of the past experience in the field of speech analysis or text retrieval, some evaluation campaigns have been organized since the end of the 90's in order to create data sets which can be shared among different laboratories, to spread the costly annotation effort among all the participants, and to allow researcher to compare their ideas and contributions with sharper evaluation tools.

Basically, the first motivation is to define precise experimental frameworks. It is generally considered that experimental results are likely to be less subjective when they are obtained with largely referenced data sets, annotations and evaluation tools. The main reason is because they are supposed to be externally generated resources. Furthermore, when those resources have been already used to evaluate similar analysis tools, it eases the comparison with some state-of-the-art technologies and helps to appreciate the contribution. Having the knowledge of the corpus, the reviewing process may so take into account the ability to deal with already well-known and identified difficulties or limitations raised by data themselves.

The second major interest in evaluation campaigns stands in providing areas of discussions where problem definitions and theories can be improved on a very specific topic. Being motivated by comparing scientific works, the involved community has got to agree on common definitions or common process before submitting the results. As a lateral result, the evaluation guidelines may integrate some concept or technology definitions in a similar way to the documents produced by normalization bodies. These guidelines may also identify problems of interest which may durably influence works in the corresponding domain at a large scale. But those documents are not the only outputs of evaluation campaigns which are considered of interest. The annotated data are important resources for supervised recognition tools. When they cannot be the support for some evaluation any longer, they can be offered a second life as training resources in classification processes. Here again, the fact that the training data set is well known represents an appreciated benefit to understand the scientific contribution in the recognition tool development.

Obviously, the main expected output of an evaluation campaign stands in the identification of the best technologies to address a specific task. This generally consists in ranking results thanks to some predefined metrics. This gives an overview of the potentiality in the scientific domain and allows generating a useful and relevant state-of-the-art where all proposed methods can be compared and analyzed through their ability to address some difficulties or their limitations. But another important result is the observation of the technology domain evolution year after year. When an evaluation campaign can be organized as a recurring event, offering each time a similar evaluation framework (similar data, same evaluation tools) to the participant community, it allows observing in which way the technology evolves and when it reaches its highest point. We can also observe how tasks are slightly redefined each time in order to enlarge the problem, giving so an idea of progresses along the time.

6.2 Organizing an evaluation campaign

In the following paragraphs, we present different concepts or principles used in evaluation campaigns. We may assume that each campaign proposes different mechanisms. We do not pretend to be exhaustive here. We just present a list of general principles which are likely to be the most transversal ones.

6.2.1 Organization

Different tasks have to be managed during the organization of an evaluation campaign. Members of the organizing committee are generally requested to be neutral towards the challenges. They shall not give some orientations (in tasks, annotation formats or metric definitions) which could a priori emphasize a given technology or penalize another one. Of course, they are usually not expected to be participant as well, or only with some strong restrictions. The organizing committee is in charge of writing the "organization plan" gathering all the guidelines about the evaluation paradigm which is distributed to participants. Among all the roles to be played inside the Organizing Committee should figure:

- the data providers: their role is to collect a set of data (images, videos), to eventually reformat files in order to generate some homogeneously encoded files, to manage copyright issues, to distribute or to provide an access to the content set during the campaign.
- the annotators: they are in charge of creating the annotation "ground truth" which will be used as a reference during the evaluation process. They also contribute to the annotation guide updates in adding all remarks and decision taken for the annotation of ambiguous cases.
- the evaluators are in charge of the metric definitions and of the development of the corresponding evaluation tools.
- the integrators gather and handle evaluation tools. They may also develop a web site offering services for the campaign management (participant registration, data distribution, repository where results can be uploaded, results format checking, forum, etc)
- the result editors are in charge of analyzing results sent by participants. They are expected to provide a synthetic publication intended to the participants and the evaluation campaign organizers.

6.2.2 Terminology

Many words used in evaluation campaigns on image and video analysis tools are coming from other domains, mainly text and speech where we observe a longer experience in building framework to compare technologies. This terminology is not fixed by some official dictionary, but formal definitions of some pieces of vocabulary are requested at an early stage of the process to avoid confusing situations. A typical example stands in what can be identified by the term "results". One may consider that it represents the data sent back by the participants, submitted to the evaluation process. One may consider that it designates the output of the evaluation process, i.e. the values generated by the evaluation metrics. Hereafter is a short glossary of some terms often used in that domain.

- Assessment: after the evaluation process, some elements may raise some previously unidentified issues. It can be due to some errors in the annotation. It can be due to some ambiguous cases. This may lead to a specific adjudication by the organizing committee and to apply a new evaluation step while taking into account this decision.
- Baseline: this term designates results generated by a simple state-of-the-art analysis tool. Those results are evaluated as regular ones and are used to observe how far the evaluated technologies from this basic tool are.
- Dry run: First evaluation round to identify potential problems or limitations in the evaluation process. Results coming from the dry run are not taken into account. Hypothesis may be degraded data in order to check the robustness of the evaluation tools.
- Reference: this term designates the manual annotations of the content set. The reference can be seen as the ground truth to which results submitted by participants will be compared.
- System or Hypothesis: both terms can be found in the literature to designate values submitted by the participants.
- Results: without any other precision, results are generally associated to ranks or error rates or the output of any metric used to evaluate technologies in the evaluation guidelines.
- Run: this corresponds to one hypothesis built with the output of one analysis tool applied in the same conditions to all the content set files (same parameters values, same training data sets, etc). During an evaluation campaign, a predefined fixed number of runs may be submitted by participants. It allows them to test different analysis tools, or different sets of parameters for a same tool.

6.2.3 Agenda

A typical agenda for an evaluation follows these steps:

1. tasks, content set, formats, metrics definition
2. round table with participants: this steps aims at verifying that there is a common agreement and a good understanding of the evaluation process
3. content set, annotation, evaluation tools production.
4. dry run organization

   - development data, evaluation tool distribution: development data are supposed to be representative of the content set. These resources are generally required to train supervised recognition tools. They can be also used to determine the best parameter values for generic analysis tools to obtain the best results for a specific content set.
   - test data distribution: Data used as a support for the evaluation are generally distributed only at a predefined date in order to give to all participants the same amount of time to generate their hypothesis.

- hypotheses submission. They normally must respect a format which can eventually be checked during this step. The goal is to avoid unexpected errors when applying the evaluation tools, but also to prevent participants from disappointing results only due to some syntactic reasons.
- evaluation and result diffusion. The annotation used for the evaluation may also be distributed in order to let the participants check their own results.
- assessment, round table with participants. At this moment, participants can raise some observations, shortcomings, problems in the evaluation process that should be taken into account. They can also deny some of their results and explain their motivations. In the case of a common agreement, this can lead to some modifications in the forthcoming evaluation step.

5. annotation, evaluation tool upgrades: This step depends on the output of the previous assessment step and on the organizer experiences of the dry run process.
6. evaluation organization: it follows the same steps than the dry run.
7. result updates: after the second evaluation step, some updates can be still necessary in order to obtain a common agreement between participants.
8. final result publication

In case of recurring evaluation campaigns, participants can be involved the definition of forthcoming tasks. Some new tasks may be defined with a specific status in order to test the robustness of the proposed evaluation paradigm and gather a sufficiently large content set before a first real evaluation step.

6.2.4 Copyrights and legal matters on the content set distribution and exploitation

Content providers, especially in evaluation campaigns of image and video analysis tools, have often to face some limitations in data distribution due to some legal restrictions. Basically, copyright matters may limit the way the content set can be exploited. It may not be allowed to be distributed outside the scope of the current evaluation campaign. This leads to the impossibility for researchers to compare their results with the ones obtained in the framework of the campaign after the period of the campaign. The content set may not be liable to be exploited outside the scope of the campaign. In this case, there is no legal possibility to claim new results on topics which were not addressed by the campaign. Showing video excerpts or images in scientific conferences may be forbidden. For content sets dedicated to video surveillance systems, capturing video sequences with people who can be identified may also lead to some restrictive exploitation rules. In many countries, it requires a signed agreement from each appearing persons, available for a limited time period. Most of the time, those legal restriction are required to prevent from some unauthorized commercial exploitation of the content set, especially when it has been freely provided.

6.2.5 Ground truth and annotation process

Sharp definitions of concepts, objects or segments do not prevent from ambiguous cases. We generally observe the necessity to handle an "annotation guide" to register all decisions taken during the annotation process to face those ambiguous cases and to improve the consistency of annotations. Ambiguous cases may be marked as "difficult cases". A specific flag is then attached to the content in order pay a specific attention to these cases during the evaluation process. For example, results can be produced while and while not taking into account those cases. In the Clear campaigns [1], organizers decided to use two flags: "Don't Care Frames" (to exclude frames from the annotation − and so from the evaluation process) and "Don't Care Objects" (DCO) (to exclude irrelevant objects − and more precisely here some faces which could not be identified). In the Argos campaign [113], the flag "Joker" was used to identified difficult cases. Manually annotating a content set is generally a very costly process. Some strategies have been developed to reduce that cost in some cases. For example, only a subpart of the content set can be annotated. Participants are then expected to send a hypothesis covering the whole content set. But this hypothesis is only evaluated on the annotated part. Participants are not informed about the specific parts on which the evaluation will focus. If a sufficient number of participants is reached, another possible strategy to reduce the annotation cost consists in gathering the N most relevant results (when they are ranked) from all submitted hypothesis, to manually judge them and to keep only the actually relevant ones. They are then used as a reference to evaluate the so-called "inferred average precision" [230]. Here, the annotation step is performed after the hypothesis submission.

6.2.6 Evaluation metrics

Some typical metrics are inspired by those used in the information retrieval domain. In this case, the hypothesis may identify two types of data elements: positive (relevant) and negative (non-relevant) ones. Most of the times, only positive elements are returned in the hypothesis, assuming that all other are negative. When comparing the hypothesis and the reference, elements can be classified and counted in the following categories:

- True positives: a true positive is an element of the hypothesis identified as satisfying the query or as relevant for a detection task and which actually is an expected result.
- True negatives: a true negative is an element of the hypothesis identified as unsatisfactory for the query or as non-relevant for a detection task and which is actually not relevant.
- On the opposite side, false positives and false negatives correspond to error cases. False positives are elements of the hypothesis returned as positive cases while

they actually do not fit the task. False negative are omitted but expected elements or elements identified as wrong cases in the hypothesis.

These definitions may be adapted to fit actual cases for detection or identification tasks. But, they can be directly used in the following metrics:

- Recall rate: this is the number of true positives over the sum of true positives and false negatives.
- Precision rate: this is the number of true positives over the sum of true and false positives.
- The F-measure is defined as the "harmonic mean" of recall and precision. This metric is often used because it consists in a combination of the two previous metrics into a single value. It is equal to twice the product of the precision and the recall rates over the sum of the two rates.
- The Average Precision is the evaluation of ranked results (from the most to the less relevant). In practice, it is define by the following formula:

$$\sum_{k=1}^{n} Precision(k).(recall(k-1) - recall(k))$$

where k is the order number of a returned result in the hypothesis. precision(k) and recall(k) are the precision and recall rates obtained while taking into account only the k first results, recall(0) being null. In PASCAL, k takes only a subset of possible values so that the recall variation is constant (actually equal to 0.1).
- Mean Average Precision: this metric can be applied only when several tests are performed for a given task (several concept to be detected for example). It is equal to the mean of all average precisions obtained for each test.

For segmentation tasks, one may consider two different cases: one adjacent segment must be detected in a piece of the content set versus the situation where several segments must be detected. In the first case, the proposed metrics for such a task are generally computing an error rate as being the ratio between the intersection between the two segments and their union. In the second case, some segments returned in the hypothesis may overlap several segments in the reference and vice-versa. Generally, a first step consisting in matching one segment of the reference with one segment of the hypothesis is applied (see CLEAR (task on face detection and tracking), TREC 2009 (task on video surveillance event detection) for example). It may consist in associating segments with the maximum overlap when this overlap is judged of a sufficient size or duration. In case of fuzzy boundaries, one may reduce the local errors on segment boundaries by just taking into account the distance between centers of gravity.

In order to emphasize limitations of the evaluated technologies, one may define various error rates. The goal for a participant is to obtain the lowest error rate. Such metrics can be expressed on an opened scale: the lowest value is 0 while there is no limitation for the highest value. Error rates can be normalized, but in this case some attention must be paid to some possible drawbacks. To normalize the metric, it is generally necessary to divide by the number of elements in the reference and in the hypothesis. But, doing so, participants may reduce the error rate by artificially increasing the number of elements in the hypothesis. It may so not be recommended to systematically propose normalized error rates.

It is not possible to list all the metrics which have been proposed in all the evaluation campaigns on image and video analysis tools. Let us mention here as an atypical process, the one used in TRECVID 2008 on automatic summarization. Results were manually evaluated. The evaluator was asked to give a graduated rank between "strongly disagree" and "strongly agree" as an answer to a set of questions. He also had to verify that a predefined set of concepts of events can be seen in the summary. When a summary was judged by several evaluators, the mean of the given marks is used in the evaluation metrics.

6.3 Main evaluation campaigns overview

Among the periodic evaluation campaigns in visual content retrieval, TRECVID [202] is one of the main ones. Several others are also significant like Pascal VOC, ImageNet ILSVRC, ImageCLEF and MediaEval. These will be presented in the next sections.

6.3.1 TRECVID

As mentioned by the organizers on the NIST site[A]: "The main goal of the TREC Video Retrieval Evaluation (TRECVID) is to promote progress in content-based analysis of and retrieval from digital video via open, metrics-based evaluation. TRECVID is a laboratory-style evaluation that attempts to model real world situations or significant component tasks involved in such situations."

TRECVID initially started in 2001 as a track within the NIST Text REtrieval Conference (TREC) and it became an independent workshop in 2003. Over the years it covered a dozen of different tasks. Table 6.1 shows the evolution of these tasks over years. As resources are necessary for the organization of the tasks and for the assessment of the results, only a limited number of tasks, typically between two and six, can be run each year. Therefore, some tasks have to be stopped so that new ones can be started. Tasks are removed when the addressed problem is considered as solved or when no significant novelty is expected. This was the case for instance for the shot boundary detection task that was stopped in 2007 after being run for seven years. New task are introduced where novelty is expected and when progress in the domain makes new objectives appear reachable like for instance the surveillance event task introduced in 2008. Some tasks are extended for a significant number of

---

[A] http://trecvid.nist.gov

years while some lasts only one or two years like camera motion identification that was not considered very interesting.

Year	2001	2002	2003	2004	2005	2006	2007	2008	2009	2010	2011
Shot boundaries	X	X	X	X	X	X	X				
Ad hoc search	X	X	X	X	X	X	X	X	X		
Features/semantic indexing		X	X	X	X	X	X	X	X	X	X
Story boundary detection			X	X							
Camera motion					X						
BBC rushes					X	X					
Summaries							X	X			
Copy detection								X	X	X	X
Surveillance events								X	X	X	X
Known-item search										X	X
Instance search										X	X
Multimedia event detection										X	X

Table 6.1 Evolution of TRECVID tasks

The general philosophy of NIST campaigns is to evaluate complete systems like typically the ad hoc search of shots containing a given topic within a collection of video documents. System components are generally not evaluated as such because it is difficult to define a realistic and useful task corresponding to these components. Also, there is no guarantee that a method which is good by itself for such a subtask will be the most efficient within a complete system. In the case of video retrieval however, a number of subtasks were defined and evaluated separately due to the high complexity of the higher level task and to the possibility of defining meaningful subtask. While the ad hoc task remains the real use case, the following subtasks were defined and evaluated separately as components useful to achieve it. These included segmentation tasks at the signal level (shot boundary detection) and at the semantic level (story or scene boundary detection). They included also the detection of features, also low level ones like camera motion or high level ones like concepts or multimedia events.

The ad hoc search task itself was finally stopped because it was considered that it did no longer brought significant innovation even if it was not considered as solved. It was replaced by variants like the instance search (search from examples) and known item search (search for a previously seen shot or document from a description of it). A few different higher level tasks were also introduced like: detection of modified copies of video segments, video surveillance event detection, structuring of rush repositories and summarization of rush sequences.

Over the years, there has also been an evolution in the amount and in the variability of video data used for the systems' evaluation. Considering the type of data, it included TV news in English, Arabic and Chinese, rushes from BBC, documentaries in Dutch, airport surveillance videos, Internet Archive videos with creative commons license and videos from HAVIC Internet multimedia. Whenever possible, a same source of data is used for several years while new test data is added each year. Also, when possible, a same source of data is shared between several tasks and even results from one task can be used as input for another task. For instance, the results of the high level features (concepts) detection task were shared by the participants and used as indexing elements for the ad hoc search task from 2004 to 2009. The volume of data itself grew from about 11 hours of video in 2001 to about 1700 hours in 2011.

There has been simultaneously an increase also in other scalable dimensions. For instance, the concept detection task started with 10 concepts in 2002 but many participants processed only a few of them individually and it grew up to 130 in 2010 and to 346 in 2011.

The number of topics in the ad hoc task was kept stable to 25 because of the time necessary to run the interactive runs and to do the assessment of submissions but the difficulties of the queries also evolved over time so that the task remains challenging despite the technical progress over the years.

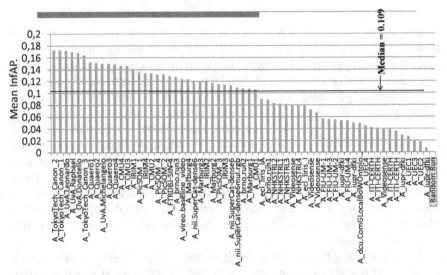

Fig. 6.1 Sample of TRECVID results for the semantic indexing full task (2011)[B]

Figure 6.1 shows a sample of TRECVID results for the semantic indexing full task (2011). Submissions are ranked according to the official evaluation measure (mean inferred average precision, estimation of the MAP). The best system had an estimated MAP of 0.173, which is quite low considering that the range is from 0 to 1 and that a perfect system would have a MAP of exactly 1. This indicates that the problem of assigning semantic tags to video segments is hard and still far to be solved.

[B] From http://www-nlpir.nist.gov/projects/tvpubs/tv11.slides/tv11.sin.slides.pdf .

The impact of TRECVID has itself been evaluated [206]. In the last decade TRECVID has involved a total of over 110 research groups from across the globe and more than 60 groups participated in 2011. TRECVID has been directly or indirectly responsible for over 2,000 peer reviewed publications with 15,000 citations, in journals and conferences so it is a sizable scientific activity and has involved over 1,100 researchers.

6.3.2 PASCAL VOC and ILSVRC

The Visual Object Classes (VOC) challenge is organized by the PASCAL Network of Excellence[C]. As mentioned on the challenge site[D], the goal of the PASCAL Visual Object Classes [62] is: to provide standardized databases for object recognition; to provide a common set of tools for accessing and managing the database annotations; and to run a challenge evaluating performance on object class recognition.

The Pascal VOC challenge has been run from 2005 to 2011. In 2011, there were three main competitions: classification, detection, and segmentation; and three "taster" competition: person layout, action classification, and ImageNet large scale recognition. Classification, detection and segmentation competitions all considered a common set of 20 classes from four categories:

- *Person:* person;
- *Animal:* bird, cat, cow, dog, horse, sheep;
- *Vehicle:* aeroplane, bicycle, boat, bus, car, motorbike, train;
- *Indoor:* bottle, chair, dining table, potted plant, sofa, tv/monitor.

The three main tasks are defined as follows:

- **Classification**: For each of the twenty classes, predicting presence/absence of an example of that class in the test image.
- **Detection**: Predicting the bounding box and label of each object from the twenty target classes in the test image.
- **Segmentation**: Generating pixel-wise segmentations giving the class of the object visible at each pixel, or "background" otherwise.

The database is of intermediate size. It contains 28,952 images, split into 50% for training/validation and 50% for testing. For the classification task, the prediction is made via a continuous score that allows sorting the test images according to their likeliness of containing the target concept. The ranking associated to this score allows evaluating the methods or systems according to the average precision metric. In 2011, the best system had a mean average precision of 78.5%.

In the large scale task (ILSVRC), organized in conjunction with the ImageNet project[E], the training, validation and test data sets contained respectively about

---

[C] http://pascallin2.ecs.soton.ac.uk/

[D] http://pascallin.ecs.soton.ac.uk/challenges/VOC/

[E] http://www.image-net.org/

1.2M, 50k and 150k images. Participants had to classify the images according to a list of 1000 categories from WordNet. Systems had to provide a list of 5 candidate categories for each of the test images. Two metrics were considered for the performance evaluation: the "flat" one is the error rate considering that the answer is correct if the reference category is within the 5 returned ones and the "hierarchical" one which takes into account the height of the lowest common ancestor between the reference categories and any of the 5 returned ones. The best system obtained a score of 0.257 for the flat cost and of 0.110 for the hierarchical cost. It was observed that both metrics ranked the systems in a consistent way.

6.3.3 Other evaluation campaigns

CLEF (Cross-Language Evaluation Forum) is a series of conferences on Multilingual and Multimodal Information Access Evaluation. ImageCLEF[F] is held in conjunction with CLEF. It is quite similar with other campaigns for the evaluation of content-based image indexing and retrieval systems but it has the specificity of additionally taking into account textual data associated to the images. For instance, the photo annotation task of ImageCLEF is a concept detection task that can be done in three different conditions:

1. Automatic annotation with visual information only
2. Automatic annotation with Flickr user tags (tag enrichment)
3. Multi-modal approaches that consider visual information and/or Flickr user tags and/or EXIF information

ImageCLEF has been conducted since 2003 and included five tasks in 2011: Medical Retrieval, Medical user-oriented, Photo Annotation, Plant identification, Wikipedia Retrieval

The MediaEval Benchmarking Initiative for Multimedia Evaluation[G] is organized by the PetaMedia Network of Excellence[H] since 2010 and is a continuation of the VideoCLEF initiative that was also conducted in the context of CLEF in 2008 and 2009. In 2011, it included six tasks: Genre Tagging, Rich Speech Retrieval, Spoken Web Search, Affect Task (violent scene detection), Social Event Detection and Placing Task (geo-localization of visual content).

The REPERE challenge[I] is organized by the French National Research Agency[J]. The goal is to find person related information in broadcasted video programs. Four tasks are defined as answering to the questions: Who is seen? Who is speaking?

[F] http://www.imageclef.org/2011

[G] http://www.multimediaeval.org/

[H] http://www.petamedia.eu/

[I] http://www.defi-repere.fr/index.php?id=27

[J] http://www.agence-nationale-recherche.fr/

Whose name is pronounced? Whose name is written? The search can be done either in the corresponding modality or in a multimodal way.

6.4 Conclusion

In campaigns on image and video analysis tools, data are distributed to participants a sufficient time before results are expected to be returned. It gives so the possibility to tune automatic tools, and even more, to authorize human intervention in the hypothesis generation process. Some evaluation campaigns on other domains (MIREX for example on musical contents) consist in submitting analysis tools to the evaluator (and not the values generated by these tools. The evaluator is so in charge of running the evaluation tool on the content set. This content set is then never sent to the participants before the assessment step. This full blind evaluation limits the possibility of human interventions in order to fit the data.

Evaluation campaigns are generally very fruitful, especially when they are repeated during several years. They permit a meaningful and objective comparison of indexing and retrieval methods as well as of some as their key components. They really contribute to accelerate the progress in the domain and they help federating the work of many research teams. Exchange of components or annotation or indexing elements across participants helps the identification of the best ones and of their best combinations.

Evaluation campaigns can be used for setting and making evolve a common research direction. Organizers, considering the feedback from the participants, have to carefully design the tasks so that they are realistic and useful, and to make them evolve to stay close to the current limitations. In TRECVID and in other periodic evaluation campaigns, tasks start, evolve and stop according to the achieved progress, to the new problems that become reachable, to the potential needs of the industry and to the interest of the scientific community.

When a domain is mature, as this is the case for multimedia indexing and retrieval, evaluation drives the progress within it; evaluation comes before the development of new methods, not after.

There is however a number of limitations associated to the practice of evaluation. First, there is an exaggerated trend to reject anything that has not been properly evaluated or that has been evaluated but with a performance currently well behind the current state of the art. This prevents the emergence of a number of innovative and potentially interesting ideas that should be given a chance to be further developed.

Second, participating to even a single task of a single evaluation campaign often require a large investment and a lot of engineering and non scientific work. Small groups usually have difficulties to step in and this is also linked to the previous point about the prevention of the emergence of new ideas. Cooperation between participants like the French IRIM initiative [54] can help reducing this effect.

Third, there is a trend to over tune a system implementing a method to the target data. As well as the differences in available computing power between the participants, the differences in available manpower for tuning the systems may mask the actual difference of performance between the underlying methods.

Finally, statistical significance has to be taken into consideration. Comparison between methods is only statistical and a ranking is always given with a probability. Randomization tests [70, 60] can be used to determine whether a difference is statistically significant or not.

While these limitations have to be taken into consideration and their effects have to be minimized as much as possible, the organization of periodic evaluation campaigns have a very strong and positive impact in the domain of multimedia indexing and retrieval.

References

1. In Rainer Stiefelhagen, Rachel Bowers, and Jonathan Fiscus, editors, *Multimodal Technologies for Perception of Humans*. Springer Verlag, Berlin, 2008.
2. ISO/IEC 15444-1:2004. Jpeg 2000 image coding system: Core coding system. *Information technology*, 2004.
3. N. Adami, A. Boschetti, R. Leonardi, and P. Migliorati. Scalable coding of image collections with embedded descriptors. In *International Workshop on Multimedia Signal Processing*, pages 388–392, 2008.
4. N. Adami, A. Boschetti, R. Leonardi, and P. Migliorati. Embedded indexing in scalable video coding. *Multimedia Tools and Applications*, 48(1):105–121, 2010.
5. M. A. Aizerman, É. M. Braverman, and L. I. Rozonoèr. Theoretical foundations of the potential function method in pattern recognition learning. *Automation and Remote Control*, 25:821–837, 1964.
6. R Albatal, P Mulhem, and Y Chiaramella. Visual phrases for automatic images annotation. In *Content-Based Multimedia Indexing (CBMI), 2010 International Workshop on*, pages 1–6. IEEE, 2010.
7. N. Aronszajn. Theory of reproducing kernels. *Transactions of the American Mathematical Society*, 68:337–404, 1950.
8. D. Arthur and S. Vassilvitskii. k-means++: the advantages of careful seeding. In *Proceedings of the eighteenth annual ACM-SIAM symposium on Discrete algorithms*, pages 1027–1035, Philadelphia, PA, USA, 2007. Society for Industrial and Applied Mathematics.
9. Escofier B. Analyse factorielle et distances répondant au principe d'équivalence distributionnelle. *Revue de Statist. Appl.*, 26(4):29–37, 1978.
10. Francis R. Bach and Gert R. G. Lanckriet. Multiple kernel learning, conic duality, and the smo algorithm. In *Proceedings of the 21st ICML*, 2004.
11. Francis R. Bach, Gert R. G. Lanckriet, and Michael I. Jordan. Multiple kernel learning, conic duality, and the smo algorithm. In *ICML '04*, page 6, 2004.
12. A. Barla, F. Odone, and A. Verri. Histogram intersection kernel for image classification. In *Image Processing, 2003. ICIP 2003. Proceedings. 2003 International Conference on*, volume 3, pages III – 513–16 vol.2, sept. 2003.
13. Stanislav Barton, Vlastislav Dohnal, and Philippe Rigaux. Similarity search in a very large scale using Hadoop and HBase. Technical report, CEDRIC-Cnam, 2012.
14. Michal Batko, Fabrizio Falchi, Claudio Lucchese, David Novak, Raffaele Perego, Fausto Rabitti, Jan Sedmidubsky, and Pavel Zezula. Building a web-scale image similarity search system. *Multimedia Tools Appl.*, 47:599–629, May 2010.

15. H. Bay, A. Ess, T. Tuytelaars, and L. Van Gool. Surf: Speeded up robust features. *Computer Vision and Image Understanding (CVIU)*, 110(3):346–359, 2008.

16. H. Bay, A. Ess, T. Tuytelaars, and L. Van Gool. Speeded-up robust features (surf). *Computer Vision and Image Understanding*, 110(3):346–359, 2008.

17. S. Belongie, J. Malik, and J. Puzicha. Shape context: A new descriptor for shape matching and object recognition. In *NIPS*, 2000.

18. S. Belongie, J. Malik, and J. Puzicha. Matching shapes. In *IEEE International Conference on Computer Vision*, July 2001.

19. S. Belongie, J. Malik, and J. Puzicha. Shape matching and object recognition using shape contexts. *IEEE Transactions on Pattern Analysis and Machine Intelligence*, 24:509–521, April 2002.

20. J. Benois-Pineau. Indexing of compressed video: Methods, challenges, applications. In *Image Processing Theory Tools and Applications (IPTA), 2010 2nd International Conference on*, pages 3–4. IEEE, 2010.

21. Kevin S. Beyer, Jonathan Goldstein, Raghu Ramakrishnan, and Uri Shaft. When is "nearest neighbor" meaningful? In *Proceedings of the 7th International Conference on Database Theory*, ICDT '99, pages 217–235, London, UK, 1999. Springer-Verlag.

22. Alina Beygelzimer, Sham Kakade, and John Langford. Cover trees for nearest neighbor. In *Proceedings of the 23rd international conference on Machine learning*, ICML '06, pages 97–104, New York, NY, USA, 2006. ACM.

23. Arnab Bhattacharya, Purushottam Kar, and Manjish Pal. On low distortion embeddings of statistical distance measures into low dimensional spaces. In *Proceedings of the 20th International Conference on Database and Expert Systems Applications*, DEXA '09, pages 164–172, Berlin, Heidelberg, 2009. Springer-Verlag.

24. A. Del Bimbo. *Visual Information Retrieval*. Morgan Kaufmann, ISBN 10 1558606246, ISBN-13 978-1558606241, 1999.

25. S. Boisvert, M. Marchand, F. Laviolette, and J. Corbeil. Hiv-1 coreceptor usage prediction without multiple alignments : an application of string kernels. *Retrovirology*, 5(110), 2008.

26. A. Bordes. *New Algorithms for Large-Scale Support Vector Machines*. PhD thesis, Université Pierre et Marie Curie Paris 6, 2010.

27. L. Bottou. Stochastic gradient descent on toy problems, 2007. http://leon.bottou.org/projects/sgd.

28. L. Bottou and O. Bousquet. The tradeoffs of large scale learning. In *Advances in Neural Information Processing Systems*, volume 20. MIT Press, Cambridge, MA, 2008.

29. Y.L. Boureau, F. Bach, Y. LeCun, and J. Ponce. Learning mid-level features for recognition. In *Proceedings of the Conference on Computer Vision and Pattern Recognition (CVPR)*, 2010.

30. Y-Lan Boureau, Nicolas Le Roux, Francis Bach, Jean Ponce, and Yann LeCun. Ask the locals: multi-way local pooling for image recognition. In *ICCV*, 2011.

31. K. Brinker. Incorporating diversity in active learning with support vector machines. *Machine Learning International Workshop then Conference*, pages 59–66, 2003.

32. A.C Carrilero. Les espacesc de reprsentation de la couleur. Technical Report Technical Report 99D006, ENST, Paris, 1999.

33. C. Carson, S. Belongie, H. Greenspan, and J. Malik. Blobworld: Image segmentation using expectation-maximization and its application to image querying. *IEEE Transactions on Pattern Analysis and Machine Intelligence (PAMI)*, 24(8):1026–1038, 2004.

34. T. Chan and L. Vese. Active contours without edges. *IEEE transactions on image processing*, 10(2):266–277, 2001.

35. C.-C. Chang and C.-J. Lin. LIBSVM: a library for support vector machines. Technical report, Computer Science and Information Engineering, National Taiwan University, 2001-2004.

36. C.-C. Chang and C.-J. Lin. LIBSVM: A library for support vector machines. *ACM Transactions on Intelligent Systems and Technology*, 2:27:1–27:27, 2011. Software available at http://www.csie.ntu.edu.tw/ cjlin/libsvm.

37. E.Y. Chang, S. Tong, KS Goh, and C.W. Chang. Support vector machine concept-dependent active learning for image retrieval. *IEEE Trans. on Multimedia*, 2, 2005.

38. O. Chapelle, P. Haffner, and V.N. Vapnik. Support vector machines for histogram-based image classification. *IEEE trans. Neural Networks*, pages 1055–1064, 1999.
39. Olivier Chapelle and Alain Rakotomamonjy. Second order optimization of kernel parameters. In *In NIPS Workshop on Kernel Learning*, 2008.
40. M.S. Charikar. Similarity estimation techniques from rounding algorithms. In *STOC*, pages 380–388. ACM, 2002.
41. K. Chatfield, V. Lempitsky, A. Vedaldi, and A. Zisserman. The devil is in the details: an evaluation of recent feature encoding methods. In *BMVC*, 2011.
42. C. Chesnaud, Ph. Refregier, and V. Boulet. Statistical region snake-based segmentation adapted to different physical noise models. *IEEE Transactions on Pattern Analysis and Machine Intelligence*, 21:1145–1156, 1999.
43. F. Chevalier, M. Delest, and J.-P. Domenger. A heuristic for the retrieval of objects in video in the framework of the rough indexing paradigm. *Signal Processing: Image Communication*, 22(7-8):622–634, 2007.
44. F. Chevalier, J.P. Domenger, J. Benois-Pineau, and M. Delest. Retrieval of objects in video by similarity based on graph matching. *Pattern Recognition Letters*, 28(8):939–949, 2007.
45. O. Chum, J. Matas, and S. Obdrzalek. Enhancing ransac by generalized model optimization. In *Proc. of the ACCV*, volume 2, pages 812–817, 2004.
46. Ondrej Chum, Michal Perd'och, and Jiri Matas. Geometric min-hashing: Finding a (thick) needle in a haystack. In *CVPR'09: IEEE Computer Society Conference on Computer Vision and Pattern Recognition*, pages 17–24, June 20–26 2009.
47. Paolo Ciaccia and Marco Patella. Pac nearest neighbor queries: Approximate and controlled search in high-dimensional and metric spaces. In *ICDE 2000: 16th International Conference on Data Engineering*, pages 244–255, San Diego, CA, 2000.
48. Paolo Ciaccia, Marco Patella, and Pavel Zezula. M-tree: an efficient access method for similarity search in metric spaces. In *Proceedings of the 23rd IEEE International Conference on Very Large Data Bases (VLDB'97)*, pages 426–435, Athens, Greece, August 1997.
49. R. Collobert and S. Bengio. SVMTorch: Support vector machines for large-scale regression problems. *Journal of Machine Learning Research*, 1:143–160, 2001.
50. C. Cortes and V. Vapnik. Support-vector networks. *Machine Learning*, 20(3):273–297, 1995.
51. N. Cristianini and J. Shawe-Taylor. *An Introduction to Support Vector Machines and other kernel-based learning methods*. Cambridge University Press, 2000.
52. Michel Crucianu, Daniel Estevez, Vincent Oria, and Jean-Philippe Tarel. Speeding up active relevance feedback with approximate kNN retrieval for hyperplane queries. *International Journal of Imaging Systems and Technology, Special issue on Multimedia Information Retrieval*, 18:150–159, 2008.
53. N. Dalal and B. Triggs. Histograms of oriented gradients for human detection. In *CVPR*, 2005.
54. Bertrand Delezoide, Frédéric Precioso, Philippe Gosselin, Miriam Redi, Bernard Merialdo, Lionel Granjon, Denis Pellerin, Michèle Rombaut, Hervé Jégou, Rémi Vieux, Aurélie Bugeau, Boris Mansencal, Jenny Benois-Pineau, Hugo Boujut, Stéphane Ayache, Bahjat Safadi, Franck Thollard, Georges Quénot, Hervé Bredin, Matthieu Cord, Alexandre Benoît, Patrick Lambert, Tiberius Strat, Joseph Razik, Sébastion Paris, and Hervé Glotin. IRIM at TRECVID 2011: High Level Feature Extraction and Instance Search. In *TREC Video Retrieval Evaluation workshop*, Gaithersburg, MD USA, dec 2011. National Institute of Standards and Technology.
55. Bennett K. P. Demiriz, A. and J. Shawe-Taylor. Linear programming boosting via column generation. *JMLR*, 2002.
56. K. Djemal and H. Maaref. Intelligent information description and recognition in biomedical image databases. In *Computational Modeling and Simulation of Intellect: Current State and Future Perspectives, Book Edited by Boris Igelnik, IGI Global, ISBN: 978-1-60960-551-3*, pages 52–80, 2011.
57. K. Djemal, H. Maaref, and R. Kachouri. Image retrieval system in heterogeneous database. In *Automation Control - Theory and Practice, Book Edited by:A. D. Rodic, INTECH, ISBN: 978-953-307-039-1*, pages 327–350, 2009.

58. K. Djemal, W. Puech, and B. Rossetto. Automatic active contours propagation in a sequence of medical images. *International journal of image and graphics*, 6(2):267–292, 2006.

59. P. Dollar, V. Rabaud, G. Cottrell, and S. Belongie. Behavior recognition via sparse spatio-temporal features. In *IEEE International Workshop on Visual Surveillance and Performance Evaluation of Tracking and Surveillance*, pages 65–72, 2005.

60. S Edgington. Randomization tests, 1995.

61. M. Everingham, L. Van Gool, C. K. I. Williams, J. Winn, and A. Zisserman. The PASCAL Visual Object Classes Challenge 2011 (VOC2011) Results. http://www.pascal-network.org/challenges/VOC/voc2011/workshop/index.html.

62. M. Everingham, L. Van Gool, C. K. I. Williams, J. Winn, and A. Zisserman. The pascal visual object classes (voc) challenge. *International Journal of Computer Vision*, 88(2):303–338, June 2010.

63. C. Faloutsos, W. Equitz, M. Flickner, W. Niblack, D. Petkovic, and R. Barber. Efficient and effective querying by image content. *Journal of Intelligent Information Systems*, 3:231–262, 1994.

64. R.-E. Fan, K.-W. Chang, C.-J. Hsieh, X.-R. Wang, and C.-J. Lin. Liblinear: A library for large linear classification. *Journal of Machine Learning Research*, 9:1871–1874, 2008.

65. J. Fauqueur. *Contributions pour la Recherche d'Images par Composantes Visuelles*. PhD thesis, Université de Versailles, 2003.

66. J. Fauqueur and N. Boujemaa. Region-based image retrieval: Fast coarse segmentation and fine color description. *Journal of Visual Languages and Computing (JVLC), special issue on Visual Information Systems*, 15:69–65, 2004.

67. L. Fei-Fei, R. Fergus, and P. Perona. One-shot learning of object categories. *IEEE Transactions on Pattern Analysis and Machine Intelligence*, pages 594–611, 2006.

68. R. Fergus, P. Perona, and A. Zisserman. Object class recognition by unsupervised scale-invariant learning. In *CVPR*, pages 264–271, 2003.

69. V. Ferrari, L. Fevrier, F. Jurie, and C. Schmid. Groups of adjacent contour segments for object detection. *IEEE PAMI*, 30:36–51, 2008.

70. R. A. Fisher. The Design of Experiment, 1935.

71. P. Forssén and D. Lowe. Shape descriptors for maximally stable extremal regions. In *ICCV*, 2007.

72. W. Forstner. A framework for low level feature extraction. In *3rd European Conference on Computer Vision, Stockholm, Sweden*, pages 383–394, 1994.

73. A. Foulonneau, P. Charbonnier, and F. Heitz. Multi-reference shape priors for active contours. *Int. J. Comput. Vision*, 81(1):68–81, 2009.

74. J. Fournier, M. Cord, and S. Philipp-Foliguet. RETIN: A content-based image indexing and retrieval system. *Pattern Analysis and Applications Journal, Special issue on image indexation*, 4(2/3):153–173, 2001.

75. Y. Freund. Boosting a weak learning algorithm by majority. *Information and Computation*, 121(2):256 – 285, 1995.

76. Yoav Freund and Robert E. Schapire. Experiments with a new boosting algorithm. In *In Proc. 13th Int. Conf. on Machine Learning*, pages 148 – 156, 1996.

77. A. Gagalowicz. *Vers un modle de textures*. PhD thesis, Universit Pierre et Marie Curie, Paris VI, 1983.

78. P. Gehler and S. Nowozin. On feature combination for multiclass object classification. In *ICCV*, 2009.

79. Peter V. Gehler and Sebastian Nowozin. On feature combination for multiclass object classification. In *IEEE ICCV*, 2009.

80. Aristides Gionis, Piotr Indyk, and Rajeev Motwani. Similarity search in high dimensions via hashing. In *Proceedings of the 25th International Conference on Very Large Data Bases (VLDB'99)*, pages 518–529, San Francisco, CA, USA, 1999. Morgan Kaufmann Publishers Inc.

81. D. Gorisse, M. Cord, and F. Precioso. Salsas: Sub-linear active learning strategy with approximate k-nn search. *Pattern Recognition*, 44:2343–2357, October 2011.

82. P.-H. Gosselin and M. Cord. Active learning methods for interactive image retrieval. *IEEE Trans. on Image Processing*, 17(7):1200–1211, July 2008.

83. P.H. Gosselin, M. Cord, and S. Philipp-Foliguet. Combining visual dictionary, kernel-based similarity and learning strategy for image category retrieval. *Comput. Vis. Image Underst.*, 110(3):403–417, 2008.

84. P.H. Gosselin, M. Cord, and S. Philipp-Foliguet. Combining visual dictionary, kernel-based similarity and learning strategy for image category retrieval. *Computer Vision and Image Understanding*, 110(3):403–417, 2008.

85. K. Grauman. *Matching Sets of Features for Efficient Retrieval and Recognition*. PhD thesis, MIT, 2006.

86. K Grauman and T Darrell. The pyramid match kernel: Discriminative classification with sets of image features. *IEEE International Conference on Computer Vision*, 2005.

87. K. Grauman and T. Darrell. Pyramid match hashing: Sub-linear time indexing over partial correspondences. *CVPR*, pages 1–8, 2007.

88. L. Guigues, J.P. Cocquerez, and H. Lemen. Scale-sets image analysis. *International Journal of Computer Vision*, 68(3):289–317, 2006.

89. I. Guyon, B. Boser, and V. Vapnik. Automatic capacity tuning of very large VC-dimension classifiers. In *Advances in Neural Information Processing Systems*, volume 5. Morgan Kaufmann, 1993.

90. E. Hadjidemetriou, M.D. Grossberg, and S.K. Nayar. Multiresolution histograms and their use for recognition. *IEEE Transactions of Pattern Analysis Machine Intelligence*, 26(7):831–847, 2004.

91. J. Hafner, H. Sawhney, W. Equitz, M. Flickner, and W. Niblack. Efficient color histogram indexing for quadratic form distance functions. *IEEE Trans. Pattern Anal. Mach. Intell*, pages 729–736, 1995.

92. Stefano Soatto Haibin Ling, H Ling, and S Soatto. Proximity distribution kernels for geometric context in category recognition. In *International Conference on Computer Vision*, pages 1–8. IEEE, October 2007.

93. R. M. SK. Haralick and I. Dinstein. Textural features for image classification. *IEEE Transactions on Systems, Man and Cybernetics*, 232:610–621, 1973.

94. C. Harris and M. Stephens. A combined corner and edge detector. In *Alvey Vision Conference*, pages 147–151, 1988.

95. J.-E. Haugeard, S. Philipp-Foliguet, and F. Precioso. Windows and facades retrieval using similarity on graph of contours. In *IEEE International Conference on Image Processing (ICIP 09)*. Citeseer, November 2009.

96. Jean-Emmanuel Haugeard, Sylvie Philipp-Foliguet, Frédéric Precioso, and Justine Lebrun. Extraction of windows in facade using kernel on graph of contours. In Arnt-Børre Salberg, Jon Yngve Hardeberg, and Robert Jenssen, editors, *Image Analysis*, volume 5575 of *LNCS*, pages 646–656. Springer, 2009.

97. J. Hayes and A. Efros. Scene completion using millions of photographs. In *SIGGRAPH*, 2007.

98. Steven C.H. Hoi, Rong Jin, Jianke Zhu, and Michael R. Lyu. Semi-supervised svm batch mode active learning for image retrieval. In *IEEE CVPR*, pages 1–7, 2008.

99. R. Horaud, T. Skordas, and F. Veillon. Finding geometric and relational structures in an image. In *1st European Conference on Computer Vision*, pages 374–384, 1990.

100. Michael Houle, Hans-Peter Kriegel, Peer Kröger, Erich Schubert, and Arthur Zimek. Can shared-neighbor distances defeat the curse of dimensionality? In Michael Gertz and Bertram Ludäscher, editors, *Scientific and Statistical Database Management*, volume 6187 of *Lecture Notes in Computer Science*, pages 482–500. Springer Berlin / Heidelberg, 2010.

101. J. Huang, S. R. Kumar, M. Mitra, W. J. Zhu, and Zabih R. Image indexing using color correlograms. In *Computer Vision and Pattern Recognition, IEEE Computer Society Conference on*, pages 762–768, 1997.

102. J. Huang, S. R. Kumar, M. Mitra, W. J. Zhu, and Zabih R. Spatial color indexing and applications. In *International Conference on Computer Vision*, volume 35, pages 245–268, 1999.

103. T.S. Huang, C.K. Dagli, S. Rajaram, E.Y. Chang, M.I. Mandel, G.E. Poliner, and D.P.W. Ellis. Active learning for interactive multimedia retrieval. *Proceedings of the IEEE*, 96(4):648, 2008.

104. Piotr Indyk and Nitin Thaper. Fast Image Retrieval via Embeddings. In *3rd International Workshop on Statistical and Computational Theories of Vision*. ICCV, 2003.

105. R. Tibshirani J. Friedman, T. Hastie. Special invited paper. additive logistic regression: A statistical view of boosting. 28(2):337–374, 2000.

106. Tommi Jaakkola and David Haussler. Exploiting generative models in discriminative classifiers. In *In Advances in Neural Information Processing Systems 11*, pages 487–493. MIT Press, 1998.

107. H. Jegou, M. Douze, and C. Schmid. Hamming embedding and weak geometric consistency for large scale image search. In *European conference on computer vision*, pages 304–317. Springer, 2008.

108. H. Jégou, M. Douze, C. Schmid, and P. Pérez. Aggregating local descriptors into a compact image representation. In *CVPR*, pages 3304–3311, 2010.

109. T. Joachims. Making large-scale SVM learning practical. In *Advances in Kernel Methods – Support Vector Learning*, pages 169–184. MIT Press, 1999.

110. T. Joachims. Training linear svms in linear time. In *Proceedings of the ACM Conference on Knowledge Discovery and Data Mining (KDD06)*. ACM Press, 2006.

111. Alexis Joly and Olivier Buisson. A posteriori multi-probe locality sensitive hashing. In *MM '08: Proceeding of the 16th ACM international conference on Multimedia*, pages 209–218, New York, NY, USA, 2008. ACM.

112. Alexis Joly and Olivier Buisson. Random maximum margin hashing. In *The 24th IEEE Conference on Computer Vision and Pattern Recognition, CVPR 2011, Colorado Springs, CO, USA, 20-25 June 2011*, pages 873 880. IEEE, 2011.

113. Philippe Joly, Jenny Benois-Pineau, Ewa Kijak, and Georges Quénot. The ARGOS campaign: Evaluation of Video Analysis Tools. *Signal Processing : Image Communication*, 22(7-8):705–717, 2007.

114. B. Julesz, E. Gilbert, and J.D. Victor. Visual discrimination of textures with identical third-order statistics. *Biological Cybernetics*, 31:137–140, 1978.

115. B. Julezs. Experiments in the visual perception of texture. *Scientific American*, 232:2–11, 1975.

116. R. Kachouri, K. Djemal, and H. Maaref. Multi-model classification method in heterogeneous image databases. *Pattern Recognition*, 43(12):4077–4088, 2010.

117. S. Karaman, J. Benois-Pineau, R. Mégret, and A. Bugeau. Multi-layer local graph words for object recognition. *Advances in Multimedia Modeling: 18th International Conference, MMM 2012, Klagenfurt, Austria, January 4-6, 2012, Proceedings*, 7131:29–39, 2011.

118. Norio Katayama and Shin'ichi Satoh. The sr-tree: An index structure for high-dimensional nearest neighbor queries. In Joan Peckham, editor, *SIGMOD 1997: Proceedings ACM SIGMOD International Conference on Management of Data*, pages 369–380. ACM Press, 1997.

119. Marius Kloft, Ulf Brefeld, Soeren Sonnenburg, Pavel Laskov, Klaus-Robert Müller, and Alexander Zien. Efficient and accurate lp-norm multiple kernel learning. In *NIPS*, pages 997–1005, 2009.

120. G. Koepfler, C. Lopez, and J. M. Morel. A multiscale algorithm for image segmentation by variational method. *SIAM Journal on Numerical Analysis*, 31(1):282–380, 1994.

121. Brian Kulis and Kristen Grauman. Kernelized locality-sensitive hashing for scalable image search. In *IEEE International Conference on Computer Vision (ICCV*, pages 2130–2137, 2009.

122. I. Laptev. On space-time interest points. *International Journal on Computer Vision*, 2:107–123, 2005.

123. I. Laptev and T. Lindeberg. Space-time interest points. In *International Conference on Computer Vision*, pages 432–439, 2003.

124. I. Laptev and T. Lindeberg. Local descriptors for spatio-temporal recognition. In *First International Workshop on Spatial Coherence for Visual Motion Analysis, LNCS, Springer*, 2004.

125. I. Laptev, M. Marszalek, C. Schmid, and B. Rozenfeld. Learning realistic human actions from movies. In *Computer Vision and Pattern Recognition, IEEE Computer Society Conference on*, pages 1–8, 2008.

126. S Lazebnik, C Schmid, and J Ponce. Beyond bags of features: Spatial pyramid matching for recognizing natural scene categories. In *Computer Vision and Pattern Recognition, 2006 IEEE Computer Society Conference on*, volume 2, pages 2169–2178. Ieee, 2006.

127. F. Lecellier, J. Fadili, S. Jehan-Besson, G. Aubert, M. Revenu, and E. Saloux. Region-based active contours with exponential family observations. *Journal of Mathematical Imaging and Vision*, 36(1):28–45, 2010.

128. H Li, E Kim, X Huang, and L He. Object matching with a locally affine-invariant constraint. In *Computer Vision and Pattern Recognition (CVPR), 2010 IEEE Conference on*, pages 1641–1648. IEEE, 2010.

129. X. Li, C. Wu, C. Zach, S. Lazebnik, and J.-M. Frahm. Modeling and recognition of landmark image collections using iconic scene graphs. In *ECCV*, 2008.

130. Ruei-Sung Lin, David A. Ross, and Jay Yagnik. Spec hashing: Similarity preserving algorithm for entropy-based coding. In *IEEE Computer Society Conference on Computer Vision and Pattern Recognition (CVPR)*, pages 848–854, San Francisco, USA, June 2010.

131. T. Lindeberg. Scale-space theory: A basic tool for analysing structures at different scales. *Journal of Applied Statistics, (Supplement on Advances in Applied Statistics: Statistics and Images: 2)*, 21(2):224–270, 1994.

132. T. Lindeberg. Feature detection with automatic scale selection. *IJCV*, 30, 1998.

133. Lingqiao Liu, Lei Wang, and Xinwang Liu. In defense of soft-assignment coding. In *ICCV*, 2011.

134. D. Lowe. Distinctive image features from scale-invariant keypoints. *International Journal on Computer Vision (IJCV)*, 2(60):91–110, 2004.

135. Qin Lv, William Josephson, Zhe Wang, Moses Charikar, and Kai Li. Multi-probe LSH: efficient indexing for high-dimensional similarity search. In *VLDB'07: Proceedings of the 33rd international conference on Very large data bases*, pages 950–961. VLDB Endowment, 2007.

136. Siwei Lyu. Mercer kernels for object recognition with local features. In *Proceedings of the IEEE Computer Society International Conference on Computer Vision and Pattern Recognition (CVPR)*, pages 223–229, 2005.

137. W.Y. Ma and BS Manjunath. Netra: A toolbox for navigating large image databases. *Multimedia Systems*, 7(3):184–198, 1999.

138. J. Mairal, F. Bach, J. Ponce, and G. Sapiro. Online learning for matrix factorization and sparse coding. *Journal of Machine Learning Research*, 11:19–60, 2010.

139. F. Manerba, J. Benois-Pineau, and R. Leonardi. Extraction of foreground objects from an mpeg2 video stream in rough-indexing framework. In *Storage and Retrieval Methods and Applications for Multimedia*, pages 50–60, 2004.

140. M. Marszaek and C. Schmid. Spatial weighting for bag-of-features. In *2006 IEEE Computer Society Conference on Computer Vision and Pattern Recognition - Volume 2 (CVPR'06)*, volume 2, pages 2118–2125. IEEE, 2006.

141. D. Martin, C. Fowlkes, and J. Malik. Learning to detect natural image boundaries using local brightness, color, and texture cues. *IEEE PAMI*, 2004.

142. J. Matas, O. Chum, M. Urba, and T. Pajdla. Robust wide baseline stereo from maximally stable extremal regions. In *British Machine Vision Conference*, pages 384–396, 2002.

143. G. Medioni and Yasumoto Y. Corner detection and curve representation using cubic b-splines. *Computer Vision, Graphics and Image Processing*, 39:267–278, 1987.

144. K. Mikolajczyk and C. Schmid. Indexing based on scale invariant interest points. In *International Conference on Computer Vision*, volume 1, pages 525–531, 2001.

145. K. Mikolajczyk and C. Schmid. A performance evaluation of local descriptors. *IEEE Transactions on Pattern Analysis and Machine Intelligence*, 27:1615–1630, 2005.

146. K. Mikolajczyk, T. Tuytelaars, C. Schmid, A. Zisserman, J. Matas, F. Schaffalitzky, T. Kadir, and L.V. Gool. A comparison of affine region detectors. *International Journal of Computer Vision*, 65(1):43–72, 2005.

147. Y. Mingqiang, K. Kidiyo, and Ronsin J. A survey of shape feature extraction techniques. *Pattern Recognition Techniques, Technology and Applications, book, InTech*, pages 1–48, 2008.
148. F. Mokhtarian and R. Suomela. Robust image corner detection through curvature scale space. *IEEE Transactions on Pattern Analysis and Machine Intelligence*, 20:1376–1381, 1998.
149. C. Morand, J. Benois-Pineau, J.P. Domenger, J. Zepeda, E. Kijak, and C. Guillemot. Scalable object-based video retrieval in hd video databases. *Signal Processing: Image Communication*, 25(6):450–465, 2010.
150. H. P. Moravec. Towards automatic visual obstacle avoidance. In *5th International Joint Conference on Artificial Intelligence, Cambridge, Massachusetts, USA*, page 584, 1977.
151. P. Moreels and P. Perona. Evaluation od features detectors and descriptors based on 3d objects. *International journal of computer vision*, 73(3):263–284, 2007.
152. MPEG7. Iso/iec jtc1/sc29/wg11. Technical report, Tech. Report, 2010.
153. Yadong Mu, Jialie Shen, and Shuicheng Yan. Weakly-supervised hashing in kernel space. In *23rd IEEE Conference on Computer Vision and Pattern Recognition (CVPR)*, pages 3344–3351, San Francisco, CA, USA, 2010.
154. Yadong Mu and Shuicheng Yan. Non-metric locality-sensitive hashing. In *24th AAAI Conference on Artificial Intelligence*, Atlanta, Georgia, USA, 2010.
155. J. Nesvadba, F. Ernst, J. Perhavc, J. Benois-Pineau, and L. Primaux. Comparison of shot boundary detectors. In *IEEE International Conference on Multimedia and Expo*, pages 788–791, 2005.
156. A. Oikonomopoulos, I. Patras, and Pantic M. Spatio-temporal salient points for visual recognition of human actions. *IEEE Trans. Systems, Man, and Cybernetics, Part B*, 36:710–719, 2006.
157. A. Oliva and A. Torralba. Modeling the shape of the scene: a holistic representation of the spatial envelope. *International Journal on Computer Vision*, 42:145–175, 2001.
158. A. Opelt, A. Pinz, and A. Zisserman. A boundary-fragment-model for object detection. In *European Conference on Computer Vision*, pages 575–588, Graz, 2006.
159. F. Orabona and L. Jie. Ultra-fast optimization algorithm for sparse multi kernel learning. In Lise Getoor and Tobias Scheffer, editors, *Proceedings of the 28th International Conference on Machine Learning (ICML-11)*, ICML '11, pages 249–256, New York, NY, USA, June 2011. ACM.
160. S. Ali P. Scovanner and M. Shah. A 3-dimensional sift descriptor and its application to action recognition. In *International Conference on Multimedia, ACM*, 2007.
161. Navneet Panda and Edward Y. Chang. Efficient top-k hyperplane query processing for multimedia information retrieval. In *Proceedings of the 14th ACM international conference on Multimedia*, pages 317–326, New York, NY, USA, 2006. ACM Press.
162. Navneet Panda, King-Shy Goh, and Edward Y. Chang. Active learning in very large databases. *Multimedia Tools and Applications*, 31(3):249–267, 2006.
163. O. Pele and M. Werman. A linear time histogram metric for improved sift matching. In *ECCV*, 2008.
164. O. Pele and M. Werman. The quadratic-chi histogram distance family. In *ECCV*, 2010.
165. F. Perronnin and C. Dance. Fisher kernels on visual vocabularies for image categorization. In *IEEE Conference on Computer Vision and Pattern Recognition, 2007. CVPR'07*, pages 1–8, 2007.
166. J Philbin, O Chum, M Isard, J Sivic, and A Zisserman. Object retrieval with large vocabularies and fast spatial matching. In *2007 IEEE Conference on Computer Vision and Pattern Recognition*, pages 1–8, 2007.
167. D. Picard and P.H. Gosselin. Improving image similarity with vectors of locally aggregated tensors. In *ICIP*, 2011.
168. David Picard, Nicolas Thome, and Matthieu Cord. An efficient system for combining complementary kernels in complex visual categorization tasks. In *ICIP*, pages 3877–3880, 2010.
169. A. Pikaz and I. Dinstein. Using simple decomposition for smoothing and feature point detection of noisy digital curves. *IEEE Transactions on Pattern Analysis and Machine Intelligence*, 16:808–813, 1994.

170. J. Platt. Fast training of support vector machines using sequential minimal optimization. In *Advances in Kernel Methods – Support Vector Learning*, pages 185–208. MIT Press, 1999.
171. Sébastien Poullot, Michel Crucianu, and Olivier Buisson. Scalable mining of large video databases using copy detection. In *MM'08: Proceedings of the 16th ACM international conference on Multimedia*, pages 61–70, New York, NY, USA, 2008. ACM.
172. Sébastien Poullot, Michel Crucianu, and Shin'ichi Satoh. Indexing local configurations of features for scalable content-based video copy detection. In *LS-MMRM: 1st Workshop on Large-Scale Multimedia Retrieval and Mining, in conjunction with 17th ACM international conference on Multimedia*, pages 43–50, New York, NY, USA, 2009. ACM.
173. Rouhollah Rahmani, Sally A. Goldman, Hui Zhang, John Krettek, and Jason E. Fritts. Localized content based image retrieval. In *Proceedings of the 7th ACM SIGMM international workshop on Multimedia information retrieval*, MIR '05, pages 227–236, New York, NY, USA, 2005. ACM.
174. Alain Rakotomamonjy, Francis Bach, Stephane Canu, and Yves Grandvalet. SimpleMKL. *JMLR*, 9:2491–2521, 2008.
175. Alain Rakotomamonjy, Francis R. Bach, Stéphane Canu, and Yves Grandvalet. SimpleMKL. *JMLR*, 9:2491–2521, November 2008.
176. Parikshit Ram, Dongryeol Lee, William B. March, and Alexander G. Gray. Linear-time algorithms for pairwise statistical problems. In *Advances in Neural Information Processing Systems 22: 23rd Annual Conference on Neural Information Processing Systems 2009. Proceedings of a meeting held 7-10 December 2009, Vancouver, British Columbia, Canada*, pages 1527–1535, 2009.
177. Jerome Revaud, Guillaume Lavoué, Ariki Yasuo, Atilla Baskurt, and Université De Lyon. Scale-invariant proximity graph for fast probabilistic object recognition. In *Proceedings of the ACM International Conference on Image and Video Retrieval - CIVR '10*, page 414, New York, New York, USA, July 2010. ACM Press.
178. John T. Robinson. The k-d-b-tree: a search structure for large multidimensional dynamic indexes. In *Proceedings of the 1981 ACM SIGMOD international conference on Management of data*, SIGMOD '81, pages 10–18, New York, NY, USA, 1981. ACM.
179. N. Roy and A. McCallum. Toward optimal active learning through sampling estimation of error reduction. In *Proceedings of the Eighteenth International Conference on Machine Learning*, pages 441–448, 2001.
180. Y. Rubner, C. Tomasi, and L.J. Guibas. The earth movers distance as a metric for image retrieval. *International Journal of Computer Vision*, 40:99–121, 2000.
181. Y. Rui, T.S. Huang, M. Ortega, and S. Mehrotra. Relevance feedback: A power tool for interactive content-based image retrieval. *IEEE Transactions on circuits and systems for video technology*, 8(5):644–655, 1998.
182. H Sahbi, J Y Audibert, and R Keriven. Context-dependent kernels for object classification. *IEEE transactions on pattern analysis and machine intelligence*, pages 699–708, 2010.
183. H. Sahbi, J.Y. Audibert, J. Rabarisoa, and R. Keriven. Robust matching and recognition using context-dependent kernels. In *Proceedings of the 25th international conference on Machine learning*, pages 856–863. ACM, 2008.
184. Ruslan Salakhutdinov and Geoffrey Hinton. Semantic hashing. *Int. J. Approx. Reasoning*, 50:969–978, July 2009.
185. Hanan Samet. *Foundations of Multidimensional and Metric Data Structures*. Morgan Kaufmann Publishers Inc., San Francisco, CA, USA, 2006.
186. B. Schiele and J.L. Crowley. Object recognition using multidimensional receptive field histograms. *LNCS*, pages 610–619, 1996.
187. C. Schmid, R. Mohr, and Bauckhage C. Evaluation of interest point detectors. *International Journal of Computer Vision*, 37:151–172, 2000.
188. B. Schölkopf and A. J. Smola. *Learning with Kernels*. MIT Press, 2002.
189. C. Schuldt, I. Laptev, and Caputo B. Recognizing human actions: A local svm approach. In *International Conference on Pattern Recognition*, pages 36–36, 2004.
190. Arturo Serna. Implementation of hierarchical clustering methods. *Journal of computational physics*, 129, 1996.

191. N. Serrano, A. E. Savakisb, and J. Luoc. Improved scene classification using efficient low-level features and semantic cues. *Pattern Recognition*, 37:1773–1784, 2004.
192. J. A. Sethian. Level set methods. In *Cambridge University Press, Cambridge*, 1996.
193. M. Shahiduzzaman, D. Zhang, and G. Lu. Improved spatial pyramid matching for image classification. In *Asian Conference on Computer Vision*, pages 449–459, 2010.
194. S. Shalev-Shwartz, Y. Singer, and N. Srebro. Pegasos: Primal estimated subgradient solver for SVM. In *Proceedings of the 24th International Conference on Machine Learning (ICML07)*. OmniPress, 2007.
195. L.G. Shapiro and R.M. Haralick. Structural descriptions and inexact matching. *Pattern Analysis and Machine Intelligence, IEEE Transactions on*, (5):504–519, 1981.
196. J. Shawe-Taylor and N. Cristianini. *Kernel methods for Pattern Analysis*. Cambridge University Press, ISBN 0-521-81397-2, 2004.
197. John Shawe-Taylor and Nello Cristianini. *Kernel Methods for Pattern Analysis*. Cambridge University Press, Cambridge, UK, June 2004.
198. J. Shewchuk. Triangle: Engineering a 2d quality mesh generator and delaunay triangulator. *Applied Computational Geometry Towards Geometric Engineering*, pages 203–222, 1996.
199. J. Shotton, A. Blake, and R. Cipolla. Contour-based learning for object detection. In *IEEE International Conference on Computer Vision*, pages 503–510, Beijing, 2005.
200. J. Sivic and A. Zisserman. Video Google: A text retrieval approach to object matching in videos. In *Ninth IEEE international conference on computer vision, 2003. Proceedings*, volume 2, pages 1470–1477, 2003.
201. J Sivic and A Zisserman. Video google: A text retrieval approach to object matching in videos. In *Proceedings of the International Conference on Computer Vision*, volume 2, pages 1470–1477, 2003.
202. Alan F. Smeaton, Paul Over, and Wessel Kraaij. Evaluation campaigns and trecvid. In *MIR '06: Proceedings of the 8th ACM International Workshop on Multimedia Information Retrieval*, pages 321–330, New York, NY, USA, 2006. ACM Press.
203. G. Snedecor and W. Cochran. *Statistical Methods*. Ames : Iowa State University Press, 1967.
204. F. Suard, A. Rakotomamonjy, and A. Bensrhair. Kernel on bag of paths for measuring similarity of shapes. In *European Symposium on Artificial Neural Networks*, pages 355–360, 2007.
205. M. J. Swain and D. H. Ballard. Color indexing. *International Journal of Computer Vision*, 7(1):11–32, 1991.
206. Clare V. Thornley, Andrea C. Johnson, Alan F. Smeaton, and Hyowon Lee. The scholarly impact of trecvid (2003-2009). *J. Am. Soc. Inf. Sci. Technol.*, 62:613–627, April 2011.
207. S. Tong and D. Koller. Support vector machine active learning with applications to text classification. *Journal of Machine Learning Research*, 2:45–66, 2002.
208. Antonio Torralba, Rob Fergus, and William T Freeman. 80 million tiny images: a large data set for nonparametric object and scene recognition. *IEEE transactions on pattern analysis and machine intelligence*, 30(11):1958–70, November 2008.
209. Antonio Torralba, Rob Fergus, and Yair Weiss. Small codes and large image databases for recognition. *2008 IEEE Conference on Computer Vision and Pattern Recognition*, pages 1–8, June 2008.
210. T. Tuytelaars and L. Van Gool. Wide baseline stereo matching based on local, affinely invariant regions. In *11th British Machine Vision Conference, Bristol, UK*, pages 412–425, 2000.
211. T. Tuytelaars and L. Van Gool. Matching widely separated views based on affine invariant regions. *International Journal on Computer Vision*, 59:61–85, 2004.
212. N. Usunier, D. Buoni, and P. Gallinari. Ranking with ordered weighted pairwise classication. In *the 26th International Machine Learning Conference (ICML09)*, 2009.
213. J. van Gemert, C. Veenman, A. Smeulders, and J-M. Geusebroek. Visual word ambiguity. *IEEE PAMI*, 32:1271–1283, 2010.
214. V. Vapnik. *Estimation of Dependences Based on Empirical Data*. Springer-Verlag, 1982.
215. V. Vapnik and A. Lerner. Pattern recognition using generalized portrait method. *Automation and Remote Control*, 24:774–780, 1963.

216. V. N. Vapnik. *Statistical Learning Theory*. John Wiley & Sons, 1998.
217. Manik Varma and Bodla Rakesh Babu. More generality in efficient multiple kernel learning. In *Proceedings of the 26th ICML*, ICML '09, pages 1065–1072, New York, NY, USA, 2009. ACM.
218. A. Vedaldi, V. Gulshan, M. Varma, and A. Zisserman. Multiple kernels for object detection. In *2009 IEEE 12th ICCV*, pages 606–613. IEEE, 2009.
219. A. Vedaldi, V. Gulshan, M. Varma, and A. Zisserman. Multiple kernels for object detection. In *ICCV*, 2009.
220. SVN Vishwanathan, N.N. Schraudolph, R. Kondor, and K.M. Borgwardt. Graph kernels. *The Journal of Machine Learning Research*, 11:1201–1242, 2010.
221. H. Wang, M.M. Ullah, A. Klser, I. Laptev, and C. Schmid. Evaluation of local spatio-temporal features for action recognitio. *Methods, Computer and Information Science*, 2009.
222. Jun Wang, Sanjiv Kumar, and Shih-Fu Chang. Semi-supervised hashing for scalable image retrieval. In *IEEE Computer Society Conference on Computer Vision and Pattern Recognition (CVPR)*, page 34243431, San Francisco, USA, June 2010.
223. Yair Weiss, Antonio Torralba, and Rob Fergus. Spectral hashing. In D. Koller, D. Schuurmans, Y. Bengio, and L. Bottou, editors, *Advances in Neural Information Processing Systems 21*, pages 1753–1760. 2009.
224. G. Willems, T. Tuytelaars, and Van Gool L. An efficient dense and scale-invariant spatio-temporal interest point detector. In *ECCV*, 2008.
225. J. Wu. *Rotation Invariant Classification of 3D Surface Texture Using Photometric Stereo*. PhD thesis, Heriot-Watt University, 2003.
226. Chuan Xiao, Wei Wang, Xuemin Lin, Jeffrey Xu Yu, and Guoren Wang. Efficient similarity joins for near-duplicate detection. volume 36, pages 15:1–15:41, New York, NY, USA, August 2011. ACM.
227. Fei Yan, Krystian Mikolajczyk, Josef Kittler, and Muhammad Tahir. A comparison of l1 norm and l2 norm multiple kernel svms in image and video classification. *CBMI, International Workshop on*, 0:7–12, 2009.
228. J. Yang, K. Yu, Y. Gong, and T. Huang. Linear spatial pyramid matching using sparse coding for image classification. In *CVPR*, pages 1794–1801, 2009.
229. R.B. Yates and B.R. Neto. Modern information retrieval. *ACM P*, 1999.
230. Emine Yilmaz and Javed A. Aslam. Estimating average precision with incomplete and imperfect judgments. In *Proceedings of the 15th ACM international conference on Information and knowledge management*, CIKM '06, pages 102–111, New York, NY, USA, 2006. ACM.
231. Y.T. Zheng, M. Zhao, S.Y. Neo, T.S. Chua, and Q. Tian. Visual synset: towards a higher-level visual representation. pages 1–8, 2008.
232. X. Zhou, K. Yu, T. Zhang, and T. Huang. Image classification using super-vector coding of local image descriptors. In *ECCV*, pages 141–154, 2010.
233. X.S. Zhou and T.S. Huang. Relevance feedback in image retrieval: A comprehensive review. *Multimedia systems*, 8(6):536–544, 2003.